RITES

RITES

A Guatemalan Boyhood

Victor Perera

HARCOURT BRACE JOVANOVICH, PUBLISHERS

San Diego   New York   London

Sections of the chapter "Henry, Michael, Eduardo" first
appeared in *The Antioch Review*, Vol. 32, No. 1 and 2
(Spring/Summer, 1972) and are reprinted by permission of the
Editors. Copyright © 1972 by The Antioch Review, Inc.
Sections of "Kindergarten," "The Prodigal Uncle," "Henry,
Michael, Eduardo," "*La Revolución*," and "*Mala Saña*" appeared in
Present Tense, Vol. 12, No. 2 (Winter 1985); "Initiation" and
"Mar Abramowitz" appeared in the *Jewish Chronicle Literary
Supplement*, July 26, 1985.

Library of Congress Cataloging-in-Publication Data
Perera, Victor, 1934–
Rites, a Guatemalan boyhood.
1. Perera, Victor, 1934–   —Biography—Youth
2. Jews—Guatemala—Biography.   3. Authors, American—
20th century—Biography.   I. Title.
PS3566.E6913Z474   1986   818′.5403 [B]   86-340
ISBN 0-15-177678-4

Designed by Francesca M. Smith
Printed in the United States of America
First edition
A B C D E

For my father, in life
and in dreams

Author's Note

Names, places, and details have been changed to protect the privacy of individuals living or dead.

Contents

III
Three Returns

RITES

I

INITIATION

I WAS NOT QUITE SIX when I was circumcised for the second time because the first job, performed by a Gentile doctor, was pronounced unclean by our new rabbi. My mother tells me that a small flap of foreskin survived the first operation, so that I hung by this integument for six years between Baal and the Shield of David, a part-heathen. The ceremonial tableau has lodged in my memory, held there in trust for my understanding to ripen and draw out its full significance.

❀

RABBI ISAAC TOLEDANO, summoned from Turkey to be the first pastor of our growing Jewish community, was a man of Gothic appearance. In height scarcely above a dwarf, Rabbi Toledano bore on his back a sizable hump, but lightly, as if he was vain of it. He had raven eyes, thick brows. A black homburg perched on his large head, never a skullcap. From inside his beaked nose wiry hairs radiated like an insect's antennae.

His nose is the last thing I remember as he leaned over me, whispering unintelligible blandishments in fifteenth-century Spanish. The rest was howls, astonishing pain, the bitter sinking knowledge that I would never again be whole.

II

BOYHOOD

Father

MY PARENTS WERE BORN in Jerusalem, a few blocks from
one another, and were in their mid-twenties when they came
to the New World—Father to make his fortune, Mother several years later as his intended bride. The marriage was a
covenant between my father's Palestinian brothers and my
mother's older sister. The courtship was entirely by mail—
surface mail at that—so that pledged passions had a month
to cool on each crossing. By the time Mother arrived in
Guatemala, at age twenty-four, the bloom of their romance

had faded, and they married "for convenience," as the third cousins they were.

I was surprised to learn when we went abroad that Mother carries those letters from Father in her luggage, everywhere she goes.

☙❧

MY PARENTS WERE tradition-bound Spanish Jews, Sephardim. They both descend from a line of respected rabbis and lived their entire lives in the pre-Freudian age, as innocent of psychoanalytic theory as a rice farmer in the Punjab. I know for a certainty that neither one suffered guilt pangs when Rabbi Toledano was branding my psyche with his clippers. (When I wrote Mother about this some time ago she replied in Spanish, at the bottom of a rambling letter: "Regarding your circumcision, Jaime: You were only six years old so you suffered. Your loving mother. . . .") To them this ceremony was prescribed by the Law, which placed it beyond the soiling reach of argument or reflection, much less remorse. I wish to record, however, in defense of my own flesh and blood, that they did betray a sincere and reassuring concern when it appeared that my genital growth had been arrested, perhaps permanently, by that second mutilation. They lost no time in bundling me off to Doctor Machado—the same Doctor Machado who bungled the first job, may his name and memory be erased—to ask if he had something to make the little bird grow. I forget what Doctor Machado prescribed, but it did not take effect for another ten years. I was seventeen the morning I stumbled into the bathroom half-asleep and startled Father straight up from the toilet seat with a full-grown erection.

FATHER WAS THE middle one of three brothers who shipped to America in the 1920s to pick the gold from the paving stones. In Jerusalem, Father had been a Talmudic scholar and mathematics instructor at a girls' seminary. In Guatemala he began life as an itinerant peddler. (Why Guatemala? Father never explained this to my satisfaction.) Only recently have I come to appreciate the courage this required of him—an educated man of twenty-five, scion of respected rabbis and with only a few phrases of Quixotesque Ladino Spanish, reduced to peddling bolts of colored gingham to Indian laborers in a country so ignorant of his lineage it labeled him Turk and levied on his head double and triple the going rate in bribes, kickbacks, police taxes, and the other routine forms of graft.

And yet he grew to love his work. He took pride in his hard-earned position as one of Guatemala's leading merchants and in his standing within the Jewish community as a loyal Zionist, a scholar, and a humanist.

Some years ago I came across a yellowed photograph of Father standing at the door of his textiles shop the day it opened. The proud aura of ownership lights up his face. Father was to marry that store and consecrate his heart and mind to it with Talmudic ardor. Ourselves, his family, he fed, roofed, clothed, bedded down at night from an inherited reflex of duty. He had no real love for us.

Father was thirty-six when I was born, and nearly forty before I recognized him as my sire. By then the cares of business and advancing age had scored his brow and pinched his cheeks. I hero-worshiped Father from the start, as if from a premonition that his sway on my life would be brief. Any casual praise from him or word of advice stuck to my mind like a fly to flypaper.

The first story he told me was the La Fontaine fable of the lion and the mouse. The second was the boy who cried wolf.

A phrase that made a deep impression he spoke not to me but to a friend of his, as we strolled in the park: "The war will be good for business," Father said.

On another stroll with this same friend they discussed what private school I should go to. (Only the poor went to public school.) Father wanted a place where English was taught as a second language. "English is the most important language in the world today," I recall his saying.

When I was four Father's appendix burst and he had an emergency operation in his bedroom. His cries of pain ("Ay! Ay! Ay, Mama! Ay, Mama!") filled the house and rang in my ears for weeks afterward. More terrible than his titanic agony was the realization that titans, too, cried after their mothers.

With a boy-child's instinct I hoarded these proofs of Father's manliness:

His impressive phallus. It was deep-veined and thick, not overlong, a bull's neck crowned with all the totemic attributes of godhead. From this parent trunk his testicles hung like swollen fruit.

His gargantuan appetite. At the breakfast table I looked on in awed wonder as he drew and quartered a whole papaya and gobbled it down, block by block. (Years later I learned Doctor Machado had prescribed this daily papaya for his poor digestion.)

His enormous size. At five-and-a-half feet Father towered

four inches above Mother and six inches above most of his female employees. (This illusion vanished forever the day Uncle Mair arrived from Mexico with his new bride, Aunt Renee. Both were taller than Father by almost a head, and Uncle Mair was markedly bigger around the chest and shoulders.)

His superhuman strength. This was evidenced by the ease with which he unscrewed jam and cookie jars, unstuck windows, raised and lowered the steel shutters outside the store twice a day. A special niche was carved on my pantheon the day I sat in his boat as he outrowed five of his male employees across Lake Amatitlán. (Was that race thrown, I ask myself after all these years, to flatter a vain boss?)

The manly way he rocked on the balls of his feet during the Sabbath services. His mere presence in the synagogue was imbued with patriarchal virility and mystery, so that in this setting his lightest pat on my head acquired a transcendent significance.

His paternal counsel and admonitions. The first I remember was: "The time will come when you have to lie to strangers. But never, never lie to your mother and me." His second admonition, or rather warning, after my pedal-car was stolen for the third time, was that I was too soft and pampered, and the world would take advantage of me. (That first commandment of his I broke before my next birthday, but I took the warning to heart.)

His position of authority at home and in business. Father's rule in the home was unchallenged, at least in front of the children. He gave orders to Mother, who in turn gave orders to the cook, to my *china* (nanny), and to the two cleaning maids, Micaela of the "interior," who made the beds, and

Eulalia of the "exterior," who swept the hallway. What took place in the bedroom, behind closed doors, was on a different plane of reality and I discounted it, although from my room I overheard quarrels in which Father did not always get in the last word.

The store was Father's true domain. He had twenty-five employees at his beck and call, all but six female; about a dozen of these looked upon him with an adoration far beyond the requisites of personnel loyalty. Edna, a pretty sixteen-year-old salesgirl of Mayan descent, was my own personal favorite. Father sent her to my bedside whenever I took sick, and she would tell me ghost stories. Once, when I was racked with coughs, pretty Edna placed her hand on my groin, which had a marvelously soothing effect.

I well remember the beatings Father gave me. A restrained capacity for violence ranked high among my standards of manliness long before I got hooked on war films and comic books. Father beat me only three times in my life, in each instance with sufficient provocation, and the logic of the punishment—if not the severity—was perfectly clear to me. What makes them distinct in my mind is the gap in each case between my expectation (or lack of it) and the physical weight and texture of the beating.

The first time, he struck me because I'd left my schoolbag on a bus. This was not sufficient cause in itself and I'm sure he would have forgotten the whole thing if I had let him. He hit me because I whined when confronted with the loss, and tried to weasel out of my guilt in a cowardly way. The slap was tremendous, a cosmic detonation that flung me across the floor. It was the sound of that slap, more than the burning in my cheek, that astonished and froze my tears for several seconds.

The second time came when I traced muddy handprints on the walls after making mud pies on the patio for my baby-sister. Then my astonishment sprang from the discrepancy between the misdeed and the punishment. I had often got away with far worse offenses. But the evidence was fresh on the walls when Father got home, and, I suspect, there had been some contretemps at the store. The blow came lightning-quick, and once more I was knocked to the floor. When I pushed against the wall to get up I tracked fresh mudprints but he did not strike me again.

The third time, when I was eight years old, he beat me because I called Mother a whore. After that session I was confined to bed for nearly a week. In a sense, Mother herself was responsible for my committing that offense. It was during Holy Week, when processions passed outside our house every afternoon. I was watching one of them from my bedroom window, although Mother had specifically forbidden me to, when I felt her behind me. At that moment an image of the Virgin Mary was trooping by, wrapped in clouds of incense.

"The Virgin," Mother said, pressing my shoulder, "is a whore." She used the Ladino word *putana*.

Next time she provoked me, I flung the terrible word in her face.

I remember Mother's slow smile after I shouted the blasphemy. And yet it was not she who reported me to Father but my sister, Becky, who was barely five at the time. She remarked at the dinner table that I had called Mother a "bad name." Father, stiffening, asked me to repeat it. I flushed, lowered my eyes, my tongue stuck to my palate. He then asked Mother, and she said she didn't remember.

"What did he call you!" Father shouted, his color rising.

"*Putana*," Mother said in a low voice, as the slow smile formed on her face.

Father lifted me up by the neck with one hand and dragged me into the hallway, removing his belt. This time I steeled myself. I thought I knew what to expect. But once more reality overwhelmed my worst apprehensions.

Father took out on me a lifelong rage that evening. I still bear the scars from that strapping. But if he had not administered it I would have thought that much less of him as a father, and that much less of him as a man. That beating grew, with the years, to be one of the enduring bonds between us.

Mother

ONE OF THE UNFORGIVEN remarks Mother made to me when
I was a child was that she would have married differently—
she never said "better"—if her father had lived long enough
to afford her a dowry. "If your grandfather had lived, another
rooster would crow for me," she reminded me at every op-
portunity, unmindful that if she had married another suitor,
I might never have been born.

Mother bragged often about her father, Rosh Harabbanim
Yaakov Ohanna of Jerusalem and Samarkand. Rabbi Ohanna,
as Mother tells it, was the most learned man in Jerusalem.

He was fluent in seven languages, quoted Talmud by the yard, and was not only widely respected but loved by everyone, above all for his brimming spirits and puckish humor. Mother claims both traits, with some justice, for herself.

Grandfather, the story goes on, longed to be Chief Rabbi of Jerusalem's Sephardic community but another rabbi—connected to Father's branch of this priestly tree—stood in his way. (At this point in the chronicle Mother's face invariably darkens.) When a summons came from Samarkand for a head rabbi, Grandfather picked up his belongings and embarked alone, promising to send for his wife and children after he was settled. But then the First World War and Lenin intervened, and no word was heard from Grandfather for many months. At last he wrote to say he had remarried in Samarkand at the behest of his congregation and was raising a second family. But he vowed to return to Jerusalem after the war.

Grandfather was as good as his vow. He was en route to Jerusalem with his new family when he caught typhoid in Bombay, and soon after died. His Russian wife and two children found their way back to Samarkand alone, without having set foot in the Holy Land. (Mother threw all this up to my Hindu bride the week we were married. "Forty-five years ago my father died of the typhoid, which he caught in Bombay," Mother remarked out of the blue, to which my wife could find nothing appropriate to reply. She now thinks that an apology had been expected of her. She having failed to extend it, Mother never forgave her.)

☙❧

Her father's death when Mother was in her teens inflicted a wound that she will not permit to heal, a forever renewable sense of bright expectations forever dashed. From this un-reduced grievance Mother carved out the formula that is the bedrock of her philosophy: "The world has thwarted forever all my bright expectations; therefore, the world is forever in my debt."

Most of Mother's faults sprang from this faulty reasoning, including her chronic laziness and neurasthenia, as well as her childlike dependence on Father to make all decisions and on four servants to do everything else.

There were compensating factors to balance the ledger:

Mother had been an authentic beauty in her youth. Among my treasures is a studio photograph of her at age seventeen, taken in Jerusalem. She is sprawled on painted grass, sur-rounded by painted sheep, in a Yemenite sheperdess's blouse and skirt. Her dull cotton stockings cannot disguise the shapeliness of her legs. Her face in the photo is a perfect luminous oval framed by waist-length braids, one of those prototype cameos of maidenly sweetness that were highly prized in the twenties. I am not surprised that she was coddled and spoiled by her mother and older sisters, and pampered in his turn by Father, at least in the early years of their marriage. She would also, I imagine, have been cosseted by her Russian stepmother, had that unlucky woman reached haven in Jerusalem. (I used to have reveries about this step-grandmother of mine, raising strapping, skullcapped Bolshevik step-uncles and step-cousins on the steppes of Uzbekistan.)

The reverse side of Mother's sloth and irresponsibility was an infectious gaiety to which she gave free rein when the mood was on her, and which offset Father's abstracted sol-emnity for Becky and me. Her spirits crested on motor trips to the coast. With a kerchief around her hair to keep out the dust, Mother would toss back her head and spill out a polyglot potpourri of songs all the way to the seashore. My favorites were "La Paloma," "Sur le Pont d'Avignon," "If You Were the Only Girl in the World," and, best of all, "Mamá Inéz":

> *Ay Mamá Inéz*
> *Ay Mamá Inéz*
> *Todos los negros*
> *Tomamos café.*

(Oh Mother Inéz, all of us blacks drink coffee.)

Mother sang in a pleasant, undistinguished soprano. You could see in her face how much sweeter her voice sounded to her own ears. It was on these trips, when the gypsy in Mother came out, that I loved her best.

But she was a gypsy in other ways, not all of them so attractive. For one thing, she was childishly superstitious. Twice a month she went to Madame Fatima, on the arcade inside the Turkish Quarter, to have her fortune read in the cards. She carried on a lifelong flirtation with astrology. A Cancer, she once stayed in bed a whole week because a hostile planet was menacing her star, and she dreaded committing a fatal misstep by getting up. Despite her fluency in seven languages and top-notch schooling at a French lycée in Jerusalem, Mother was not very bright. Or perhaps it was just that she had been dependent for so long, passed in trust from one doting hand to another—grandmother to mother to aunt to older sister to Father, like a family heirloom—that she never acquired the incentive to think for herself. I once

18

gave her Ibsen's *The Doll's House* to read. She never got past Act I.

Mother's asthma was a cross we all had to bear. I suspect it was her way of punishing us for not being the golden family she might have purchased with a dowry. She went to bed every night with a man's handkerchief across her face, like a blindfold, because an Indian *curandera* assured her it would relieve the asthma. When her asthma attacks remitted, she wore the handkerchief anyway, to ward off what she called "night vapors." For extended periods Mother used the asthma as an excuse for doing nothing in the kitchen, even when guests were expected. And she wore a tight girdle as an excuse for never bending below the waist.

When Father suffered his first coronary at age sixty-one in New York, she pried into his mouth two large spoonfuls of her asthma medicine to stop his wheezing and coughing. Only my frantic call to the hospital and their prompt dispatch of an ambulance with oxygen tanks saved Father, whose lungs had to be pumped clear of water and Mother's asthma medicine.

(This was the second time I saved Father's life. The first time had been eight years before, in Brooklyn, when he suffered a cerebral stroke while sitting behind the wheel of our '51 Chevrolet. I braked the car before it rolled out of control, pushed out over my sister, Becky, who was giggling uncontrollably, and walked around to the driver's side. I gently shoved in Father, who insisted he was all right although one side of his face was pulled all out of shape and his left hand lay limp on his leg. I managed to drive the car around the block and call for help before I broke down. Father arrived at the hospital in time to be kept alive, semiparalyzed and

19

mentally impaired, for another ten years. I was seventeen that first time I saved his life, and twenty-five the second. I don't know that he ever forgave me that second time, even though it enabled him to return to the Holy Land to die.)

Mother deluded us all into believing her frail, when in reality she was strong as an ox, and Father was the frail one. Since his death in Haifa nearly twenty-five years ago Mother has not suffered, to my knowledge, an hour's breathlessness from asthma.

I have long believed it was Mother's erratic temperament that saved me from permanent crippling as a child. It's true she was intensely possessive of me, but only by fits and starts, so that I was able to elude her smothering attentions for varying intervals. (In this Chata and Elvira, my two *chinas*, helped incalculably.)

Mother kept me in shoulder-length curls well past my third birthday, and would not buy me long trousers until I started fourth grade. She persisted in dressing up my skinny frame in outlandish costumes. From firsthand report I know that she will even today whip out of her bag for a passing acquaintance in Tel Aviv a photograph of me in a black spangled mariachi outfit, age six-and-a-half, wearing a martyred grimace.

I have tended to speculate, given Mother's excessive physical interest in me, on what sort of bedmate she could have been to Father. For a long while I supposed she had to be as desultory and apathetic a lover as she was a wife and housekeeper. But one cannot presume to judge in these matters. Father was past thirty when they married, and I heard her accuse him more than once of not giving her more children. The one time I surprised them in flagrante I was too confounded by the spectacle of jointed animality, and by the ensuing uproar in the room, to store away any clues.

As I grew older I learned to use Mother, as she used me. I found I could get my favorite red Jell-O by threatening to withhold certain favors, like having my back scrubbed in the bathtub, or hitching up her pink corsets. When Rebecca was born, I would taunt, wheedle, and cajole Mother until she conceded, with a grudging smile, that she loved me "just a teeny bit more" than my mortal rival, the baby. By the time Becky was old enough to feel slighted I had lost interest in these easy victories and sought attention instead from among Father's adoring salesgirls, who were only too willing to indulge me.

Mother was fairly malleable most of the time; any boy with a moderate wit and healthy survival instincts could have handled her with ease. What made her dangerous was a wayward, unpredictable streak that surfaced years later in Rebecca in its malignant aspect, as paranoid schizophrenia.

I sometimes feel that Mother would have ended her days in a sanatorium, as Becky once threatened to, had her opinion of herself been lower, or her cunning of a higher order.

Kindergarten

MY EARLIEST IMAGES ARE geometrical: the narrow bars of the bedstead that I amazed everyone by squeezing through one windy night when I was frightened by a sheet flapping on a clothesline and wanted my mother; the perfect rectangle of Parque Central, with its octagonal tiled benches, encircled fountains, chequered flagstones. And across the way the twin towers of the cathedral, housing a dark mystery of candles and painted idols that would forever be barred to me.

In my pedal-car I explored the limits of my universe, always certain that beyond our doorstep and the park's four borders lay unnamed terrors. I was especially fond of a wooded laby-rinth in the park's northern end, a dark, sinuous place where I could act out my heroic reveries unseen by Chata, the Indian girl with long braids and sweet-smelling skirts who looked after me. To my five-year-old's eyes Chata seemed a rare beauty; she dressed in the vivid, handwoven *huipil* blouse and skirt of her region, and had unusually fine olive skin. Chata was a spirited and mischievous young woman who let me eat forbidden sweets from street vendors and who would gently tease me into fondling her firm round breasts under the thin blouse.

I made friends in Parque Central, the year before my sec-ond branding. The first I can recall was Jorge, an idiot boy with gray drooping eyes that did not disguise his sunny nature. I liked Jorge because he was affectionate—indeed, he was little else—and disarmed my budding defenses by hugging me uninhibitedly and stroking my face. Jorge taught me to touch another without shame or ulterior motive, and for this I am forever indebted to him. I grew to love Jorge and had begun to interpret his grunts and noises into a modest vo-cabulary when he stopped coming to the park. Chata found out from his *china* that Jorge had been placed in a home.

That year I acquired my first heroes, the platoon of uni-formed guards who marched past every afternoon on their way to the Palacio. I would follow them the length of the park, beating my hands to the beat of the drum, pumping my legs as high as I could to their stride. At the curb I would stop and mark time until they turned the corner and disap-peared.

Chata had an admirer, a tall Indian laborer named Ramiro who courted her in the afternoons and on weekends, when

Chata would take me to the park. Ramiro wore a straw hat and leather shoes, and used to flash a gold tooth when he smiled or smirked. Chata kept Ramiro on tenterhooks, encouraging his advances and then rebuffing him with a toss of her head, or mocking his confusion with a whinnying giggle that appeared to goad and arouse him. He looked at her at times with a cold, hungering menace that I recognized even then as lust. I disliked and feared Ramiro, but I never dared to intrude on their lovers' play or their frequent spats in the park. Instead, I would retaliate by making Chata admit, when she tucked me into bed at night, that I was her favorite.

I was some weeks short of five, and small for my age, the first time Chata took me to school and abandoned me in the hands of a tall, gaunt woman with hard eyes and a pursed mouth. Her name was Miss Hale, and I detected from her accent that she was foreign.

"Aren't we a little small to be starting school?" she said, in slow, badly slurred Spanish. I understood this to be a taunt, which, on top of my desertion by Chata, brought tears to my eyes. I feared and distrusted Miss Hale all the more when I realized this was the exact reaction she wanted, and my tears had placated her.

The room she led me into was musty and dim. I was presented to my classmates, most of whom seemed strange to me, and very large. Even their names, Octavio, Gunter, Michel, Loretta, had a foreign ring. From my earliest consciousness I had known I was a foreigner in this strange place, Guatemala. Now, in the kindergarten room of the English-American School, I felt an alien among aliens.

"My mother says you are a Jew." It was Arturo, a dark,

thickset boy with hooded eyes and hairy legs below his short trousers. Within a week he and Gunter, a tall blond boy with smudged knees who made in his pants, established themselves as the class bullies. We were at recess, which meant I could play with my new friends, plump-cheeked Grace Samayoa and Michel Montcrassi, who was French, and wore sandals on his stockinged feet and a round blue cap. There was a fountain in the patio with goldfish in it, and a rising nymph with mossy green feet who poured water from her pitcher. In each corner of the patio (Mother said it had once been a convent) was a large red flowerpot, with pink and white geraniums. I sensed the question was critical and I must reply with care.

"Yes," I said.

"My mother says the Jews killed Christ."

Now this was a trickier question. Who was Christ? "They did not," I said, but all I could be certain of was that I, at least, had not killed Christ—whoever he was—because I had never killed anyone, at least not knowingly. Then I remembered stepping on a cockroach once, and stomping on ants in the kitchen. Maybe I had killed Christ by accident.

"Prove it," Octavio said.

I told him I would ask Father about it and give him a reply the next day.

That night I asked Father why I was a Jew. He hoisted me up by the armpits, sat me on his knee, and told me a long and complicated story about God, the Bible, and a Jew named Moses. When I asked if it was true that the Jews had killed Christ he frowned and said the Romans had done it. He said I should pay no attention to Arturo.

When Arturo approached me next day Father's story had gone clear out of my head. All I remembered was that the Romans had done it.

"The Romans killed Christ," I said.

"Who are the Romans?" Arturo asked.

I said I wasn't sure, but would ask Father and let him know.

When I asked Father in the evening he was reading a newspaper. He said the Romans did it and that was that, and I was to pay no heed to Arturo. Father was not in a talkative mood, and I did not press the matter. But I was confused, and feared my next encounter with Arturo.

Several days passed, and Arturo did not mention the Jews and Christ. I dared hope the whole subject had been forgotten. In the meantime my friendship with Michel grew. He let me call him "Coco," which was his nickname, because his head was round and hard like a coconut; even his curly blond hair resembled a coconut husk. Coco was as much a foreigner in the school as I was. He was Protestant, and the bigger boys mocked his French accent and played catch with his cap.

Grace Samayoa was a little shy of me, although she liked me to tell her stories I'd made up in the labyrinth. Now and again she gave me an approving smile when I answered Miss Hale's questions correctly—and once she let me stroke her hair. Grace Samayoa was the most attractive female I knew next to Chata and my mother. But Grace was also my own size, which made her a challenge. I longed to hug her.

One afternoon Chata failed to pick me up at school. That morning Ramiro had followed us to school, as usual, although they had quarreled in the park the day before when he caught her flirting with a young chauffeur.

"He's following us. Don't turn around," I recall Chata saying, glancing behind her without turning her head. They were the last words of Chata's I would ever hear.

It had grown dark outside and my knees were cold when Father finally came for me, after closing the store.

"Chata has gone away," was all he would say. "We will get you another *china*."

After dinner I went into the kitchen and wormed the truth out of Clara, the cook. She said Chata and I had been followed by Ramiro. After she deposited me at the school he waylaid Chata a block away and gave her *"siete puñaladas en el mero corazón"* (seven knife stabs in the very heart). I accepted Clara's story on faith, not at all concerned that her description matched word for word the title of a popular song. I stamped about the house, pumping my legs high like the palace guards and chanting the song title aloud: *"Sié-te Puña-ládas en El Mero Corazón. Sié-te Puña-ládas en El Mero Corazón."* The resonance of the phrase, its hard metric beat, gave Chata's disappearance a finality I could comprehend.

The fuller import of Chata's death did not dawn on me until the following day, when I was taken to school by her older sister, Elvira, whose braids were neither as long nor as glossy as Chata's, and whose skirts did not smell half as good.

In the days that followed, Chata's violent death and Arturo's hard questions got mixed together in my dreams, and my apprehension grew that Chata had been murdered because of me, and because I was a Jew.

Unlike her younger sister, Elvira was a practicing Catholic, and one Sunday afternoon she sneaked me into the Cathedral across from the park.

"You must pray to our Lord," she whispered, pointing to

the pale naked statue, with bloodied ribs and thorns on his head, that hung with arms outstretched from the front wall, in the same place where the Ark would stand in our synagogue; only this place was a lot bigger and scarier.

When I balked at reciting the Pater Noster she had taught me, Elvira rebuked me, "You must pray to our Lord to be forgiven for your ancestors' sins against him. That way you can go to Heaven, even if you're not Catholic."

Choking back tears, I mumbled the Pater Noster, not for myself so much but for Chata, who Elvira said had been punished for her sins.

❧

DURING RECESS ONE noon Arturo again brought up the Jews and Christ. This time Gunter was with him, and there was something in his face I had not seen there before. Gunter's blue eyes never looked right at yours.

"My mother says all Jews have tails and horns," Arturo said, with an accusing look. Now this I knew was absurd, because I had seen myself in the mirror.

"They do not," I said.

"Jews have bald-headed pigeons," Gunter said, with a smirk.

I flushed, because this was true—at least I did, Father did and Uncle Mair, and Mr. Halevi at the Turkish baths, but not Señor Gonzales and the others there that day—their pigeons weren't bald. . . . But then—what business was it of Gunter's anyway?

"It's none of your business," I said. My face was hot.

"My mother says Jews are the devil," Arturo said, and gave me a shove.

Gunter called the other boys over and said, "Look at the Jew who killed Christ." Then they all gathered behind him and Arturo and stared at me.

"Leave him alone," called a thin, furry voice from the back. "He's not the devil." It was Coco.

"You keep still, dirty Frenchy," Gunter said.

"Dirty Frenchy, dirty Frenchy," chorused the other boys. Someone snatched the beret from Coco's head and they all stomped on it, one by one.

"Let's look at his bald-headed pigeon," Gunter said, turning toward me, without looking in my eyes.

I was growing frightened now, but not of Gunter, whom I suspected to be the instigator of all this. I feared the mob.

"He killed Christ," Gunter said, in a rising voice, and the group behind him grew tighter. Arturo shoved me again, harder. Torn between fear and anger, I wanted to punch Gunter in the face. But Gunter was a head taller than I, and out of reach.

I stretched to my full height. "At least I don't make in my pants," I said, and looked Gunter straight in the eye.

He made a grab for my suspenders and I swung at his face. But Arturo held me fast and then all the other boys fell on top of me. I kicked and scratched and defended myself, but they were too many. When they had stripped off all my clothes— except my shoes and socks—they stepped back to look at me.

"He lost his tail," Arturo said, almost in relief.

"But he has a bald-headed pigeon," Gunter said. A giggle came out of his face that was unlike any sound I had ever heard from a boy, or anyone else.

I turned toward the wall. My chest ached from the effort

to hold back tears. Several of the boys had drifted away, as if they wished to distance themselves from the two leaders.

Silence, except for the trickle of the fountain and the heaving of my chest. Coco came forward and offered me his crushed beret so I could cover myself.

More boys moved away and I saw that the girls had all gathered at the far end of the patio, behind the fountain—all except Grace Samayoa. She sat on the rim of the fountain, and stared at me.

"Don't look," I said to Grace Samayoa, and turned to one side. But she kept on looking.

Then Grace Samayoa said, "I hate you," and walked toward the girls at the far end of the patio.

I covered myself with Coco's cap, and I cried. I cried at the top of my lungs until Miss Hale came. She cleared everyone from the patio and told me to get dressed.

❦

THE FOLLOWING YEAR I was left back in kindergarten. Miss Hale and my parents agreed I was underage for the first grade.

Rebecca

WE WERE IN PARQUE CENTRAL the afternoon I deigned
to notice my sister's existence. Chata had sneaked away somewhere, probably to flirt with one of her lovers. I approached
Rebecca's carriage with some mischief in mind and looked
down at the perfect sleeping bundle. I was struck by her fair
skin. Becky was light blond as a child, whereas I had been
swarthy from the start.

Rising on tiptoe I reached in and tweaked Becky's nose.
She wrinkled it like a rabbit, but did not stir. I tweaked her
nose again. Becky opened her eyes and looked around, be-

wildered. When she saw me leering down at her she knitted her brows, her mouth drooped, but she did not cry. She had more spunk than I'd expected. She widened her beautiful brown eyes at me in hurt reproach.

My hand was poised to tweak her again, but the impulse died, and I chucked her under the chin instead. Becky cooed softly, and we were friends.

This first encounter set the pattern of our relationship. As we grew older my divided feelings toward Becky hardened into two distinct masks, the nice brother and the mean. Over the years this charade between us grew more persuasive. If I did something nasty like cheat Becky at checkers or snatch the drumstick from her plate, I would duck under the table and reappear as the kind brother, nearer her own age, who would commiserate with her in a soothing falsetto.

"Isn't he nasty, our older brother," I would say. "What mean tricks he plays on both of us—why, just the other day he snatched my rubber ball right out of my back pocket. . . . And you know what else he did?" And Becky would listen attentively to my story, nodding agreement, smiling through her tears.

As her good brother we played all sorts of games together. I taught her jacks, cowboys and Indians, the drill exercises from school. I told her fairy tales from Anderson and Grimm, gave her sweets when we broke a piñata at someone's birthday party. Our favorite sport was wrestling. I would lie flat on my back, and Becky would pin my shoulders to the floor with her knees. With clenched teeth and loud grunts I feigned a superhuman struggle to lift her from me. We then rolled on the floor far longer than was necessary to pin her down.

As the wicked older brother I did things so wanton and heedless I rake them unendingly on the coals of my conscience, searching without success for the key to Becky's illness, and to her deliverance.

On too many occasions I visited my own frustrations on Becky. Because she was small and accessible, Becky often bore the brunt of my stifled resentments against the adult world's offhanded cruelties. One instance I recall with special clarity. We had recently moved to our new house two blocks from the Palace, which means I was nearing six. Chata had been dead a year, and I had only recently undergone my second circumcision. Becky and I slept on opposite ends of the same room, in the railed iron beds I had squeezed out of the year before. Now I was too big for that, but not yet tall enough, or nimble or daring enough, to climb out by myself in the dark. My parents were away for the evening, the cook and the two maids had the night off. Only Elvira was home, and I now suspect she was with her lover, in some remote part of the house.

In the middle of the night I awoke with a pressing need to pee. I called my parents first, but there was no response. Then I called Elvira's name at the top of my voice, again and again, for what seemed an eternity. Finally Becky awoke and started to whimper. But Elvira still didn't come, and my need became intolerable.

I felt certain that Elvira could hear my calls plainly, but was not moved to sufficient urgency to respond. Infuriated, I dropped my pajamas and aimed a high arching stream across the room, in the direction of Becky's whimpers. My aim was good.

Elvira did appear finally, wrenched from her lover's arms not by my repeated calls or shrill laughter but by Becky's piercing, outraged wails.

※

WHEN I VISIT Becky in state hospitals, I am still two brothers to her. In the past eight years three U.S. presidents (among other grand inquisitors) have taken charge of the hospital's television and radio sets to accuse me of treason and condemn me to death. Becky defends me against these voices in her private court of justice, sometimes in a whisper, often at the top of her lungs, so that the car I take her out in for a ride becomes clamorous with contending voices.

I never know from one visit to the next which side in this continuing trial will have the upper hand that day, or whose mask—the good brother's or the wicked's—she will hang on my tense, neutral face.

Nightmares and Bogeys

THE NIGHTMARES BEGAN AFTER the second circumcision, in my second year of kindergarten. My classmates were all my own size now, but I had grown acutely shy and kept to myself. My one real friend, Coco, had been promoted to first grade and moved four blocks down the avenue to the boys' wing of the school. Behind a timid exterior I began to fashion a rich and inviolate private self.

At night I dreamed of walking naked down Sexta Avenida, Guatemala City's main street, as passersby jeered and pointed at me. Other nightmares featured a tiger-sphinx who threatened to devour me if I didn't answer his questions correctly, and a pavement that tilted or gave way under my feet, plunging me into the abyss.

But the most terrifying of all were the dreams in which God appeared, a Michelangelesque God in flowing robes and white beard who declared in clarion tones: "When I count to twelve you shall die. One . . . two . . . three . . ." At nine or ten I would start awake in a cold sweat, gasping. This dream returned at least once a year until my eleventh birthday, when it stopped. But I still awaited each approaching anniversary or New Year's Day with a mixture of dread and tingling suspense: Would God keep his word?

After my first clandestine visit inside the cathedral with Elvira, the God of my dreams grew younger. His beard turned black and a crown of thorns appeared on his head. But his message was the same.

One year God bore a distinct likeness to Lon Chaney, Jr., as the Wolf Man.

§§

MY FIRST BOGEY was Rabbi Toledano. Crouched over the prayer stand in his black homburg and long prayer shawl, silver pointer skimming the open Torah, his beaked nose jabbing the air as he rocked to and fro—he seemed not a holy man to me at all but a sinister dwarf who had been allowed through some inexplicable blunder to take possession of our temple.

Rabbi Toledano was succeeded by *El Pipo, El Sombrerón,* a long-haired beggar with atrophied legs, and *La Maciste.*

El Pipo was the faceless run-of-the-mill bogeyman who would haul you off in a potato sack if you didn't eat all your mush. I outgrew him rapidly. *El Sombrerón* had a refinement that made him more graphically menacing: He wore several large hats piled on top of his head. Elvira quelled one of my temper tantrums by slipping into our darkened room one night balancing three straw hats on her head.

"I am *El Sombrerón* and I have come to eat you if you don't quiet this instant and go to sleeeeep."

The next time she pulled that one I was on to her and flung a toy in her face. That was the end of *El Sombrerón*.

The beggar was frightening not only because his legs were crossed sticks, so that he had to swing along the sidewalk on his hands and buttocks; what raised him to bogeyman in my eyes were his cadaver face and his shoulder-length hair, which made his sex a puzzle. Elvira nicknamed him *El Sincarne*—the Unfleshed—and said he was a Lacandon Indian, one of the closest living descendants of the ancient Maya.

El Sincarne was fearless and arrogant. If you hedged at giving him a coin he would reach up and tug at your trouser pockets, cursing your miserliness in a voice so graveled and eerie it seemed to issue from a source outside himself. Once, in terror lest he touch me, I gave *El Sincarne* a crisp one-quetzal bill that Father had awarded me for top grades in English. Father lectured me on being a namby-pamby before he made up my loss.

La Maciste, too, was real, and the most formidable of all my bogeys. Unlike the beggar, who only gave the appearance of a hermaphrodite, *La Maciste* was the real thing, and a notorious transvestite as well. I knew her first as a two-hundred-pound matron who took her morning constitutionals in Parque Central. In those days she dressed habitually in a gray cotton suit, gray cap, gray knee socks, and oxfords. (Years later I discovered her alter ego in Ilse Koch, the Bitch of Buchenwald.)

La Maciste was related to President Jorge Ubico, the "benign despot" whose rule spanned the first decade of my life. Unlike her cousin, who carried on cordial relations with Washington, *La Maciste* (alias Doña Julia Quiñones) was openly sympathetic to the Nazis. For these reasons, and more, the simple threat ". . . or *La Maciste* will get you" was usually enough to ensure my soaping behind the ears and swallowing my cod liver oil.

᠙᠙

WHEN I VISITED Guatemala in the winter of 1959 *La Maciste* had gained prominence as a staunch and vocal anti-Communist ("When the Reds come, I shall be in the front ranks of my country's defenders"). To further her ambitions Doña Julia converted to male garb and renamed herself Don Julio. Her photo appeared that year in the *New York Times*. She is shown in drag in a pinstriped gray suit, her graying hair cropped close to the head. She has one massive arm around a petite secretary, whom she intended to marry. Doña Julia had a grown son from her first marriage to an obscure government official.

Influenced by Don Julio's outspokenness, President Ydígoras Fuentes—another distant cousin—appointed him minister of education that year. On the day he took office half the teachers and students in the city went on strike, and stayed away from the public schools until his appointment was rescinded.

La Maciste retired soon after from public life, reverted to Doña Julia, and wasted away from cancer, neglected but not forgotten.

The Fight

THE YEAR I ENTERED the first grade there was a change
of command in the boys' school from civilian to military. A
band of fifth- and sixth-graders had run wild and turned the
International School into "a disciplinary problem." To cope
with the emergency the trustees appointed an army lieutenant,
Hector Gonzalez, as the new principal.

I arrived too late to witness the uprising, but stories still
circulated in the drafty halls and lavatories of the rebels'
heroic triumph over authority. They had all but taken over

the school after a month-long "reign of terror"—in their own words—against administrators, teachers, and lowerclassmen. The high point of the insurrection was the alleged rape of an American teacher, Miss Seltzer, by a thirteen-year-old sixth grader. Miss Seltzer, the senior boys gave out, with the appropriate obscenities and lewd winks, was edified by the experience, to the extent that she now preferred *chapín* lovers to her own countrymen.

We freshmen attended to these reports in solemn silence, believing every word.

In his zeal to restore order Lieutenant Gonzalez turned the I.S. into a juvenile garrison. The place even looked like a barracks, with its brooding corridors and dank, enclosed patios, the grille-windowed cells that had once housed Jesuit seminarians. A school uniform was introduced, a pygmy copy of the U.S. Army khakis, right down to the khaki tie and GI cap. For third-graders and under, the trousers were cut off at the knee. We became "cadets" and took part in close-order drill each morning, from which we marched to our classes in squad formation.

The week he assumed command Lieutenant Gonzalez suspended all constitutional liberties and ferreted out the rebel leaders with the help of informers. (Father remarked at the dinner table that Guatemala's political history was being re-enacted in the I.S.) The chief troublemaker, a thirteen-year-old retardate named Heusel, was expelled without notice. A dozen others were suspended for varying periods. None of these, as they filtered back to school, looked nearly so raffish in khaki uniform, and I stopped believing in the rape of Miss Seltzer.

Among our teachers that first year were two foreigners, Miss McMillan, a blowsy Californian, and Miss Gillead, a tall, gaunt refugee from the London Blitz.

Miss McMillan was our English grammar teacher. Her pedagogical method with Underdeveloped Peoples was to tell stories.

"Now Fishy-wishy, as you all know, lived in a small pond at the edge of the deep dark woods. We *all* know what a *pond* is, don't we? *That's* right. In this pond there also lived two close friends of Fishy-wishy's, Frogsy-wogsy and Baby turtle. Now who can tell me what a *turtle* is? Raise your hands now. Tor-*tuga*, that's right. *My*, we're wide awake this morning . . ."

I don't think any of us really minded these inane fables, which we could listen to with half an ear while thinking of something else. (The dullards in the class sat out the hour in a benign haze.) We far preferred Fishy-wishy to the slavish rote-learning in our Spanish courses, and so did our best to encourage Miss McMillan. At the start of each lesson we pleaded with her to tell us if Fishy-wishy was punished for missing school, or if Frogsy-wogsy and Baby turtle made up after their quarrel. I imagine Miss McMillan saw through our deception but went along because she had as little enthusiasm for the fine points of English grammar as we did. (To her credit, we managed somehow to acquire more English than she did Spanish.)

Miss Gillead taught us Old English history, meaning the Arthurian cycle and the Chronicles. She was an intelligent woman, with a fine ear for the rhythm and pace of an English sentence. With this excellent tool she conjured up for us the poignant dramas of Canute's duel with the sea and of Alfred's visit in the peasants' hut. And she wonderfully re-created the romance of Mallory's Arthur and his court.

Miss Gillead was exceptionally tall and lean, and had about her a homely dignity that commanded respect. She never talked down, threatened, or cajoled, as our other teachers did. Her forthright manner conveyed an adult respect, if not for our intelligence, at least for our capacity to grow. Her entry in my "memory book": " 'Always turn your face towards the sunshine, and the shadows will fall behind you.' Old Persian Proverb. "

I soon became Miss Gillead's best pupil.

My enthusiasm for English did not carry into other subjects. In all my Spanish classes I was mediocre, or worse. Shyness had much to do with this. I suffered from cramps of apprehension that I might be called on to recite aloud. My fear was not that I did not know the assignment—I often did—but that my vocal cords would fail or that I would lose control of my sphincter. During my first two years in the boys' school I had frequent spells of dysentery, which undermined my confidence. Like an invalid I dragged myself from day to day, using only a fraction of my physical and mental resources.

My worst ordeal was recreation, the hour-and-a-half at noon when we were let loose in the enclosed patio to play soccer. Participation in this manly sport was obligatory. The recreation director drew up sides, assigned positions. I was usually placed in Outside Left (or Left Out), which meant I could stay out of harm's way near the sidelines for most of the game. My contribution to the contest was to crouch small against the patio wall and pray that the ball would not roll in my direction. If it did I would get rid of it at once or I would squeeze my eyes shut and leap aside lest the whirling mass of kicking boots and slashing elbows fall upon me and cut me to pieces. . . . Behind my squeezed lids I rocketed the ball across the patio in a true arc, dead between the enemy's goal posts.

I was better at absorbing discipline. At least once a week our class would be punished for harassing a teacher or for the unconfessed trespass of a single classmate. (Like concentration camps, military schools are efficient propagators of the doctrine of collective guilt.) Punishment ranged from a hundred deep-knee bends to an hour's rigid At Attention under Lieutenant Gonzalez's felt but covert scrutiny. This penance was not unduly harsh and may even have been good for our characters in the long run, but woe to the slouch who sagged on the line or did not bend his knees to the snap. He would be hounded unmercifully until he shaped up or dropped out of school. Cheats, crybabies, and malingerers brought out the martinet in Lieutenant Gonzalez, a vain, dapper man in his late twenties, with a trim mustache. He respected only tight-lipped endurance and acquiescence to one's sentence. It did not really matter if you were rowdy; it did not count against you how seriously you offended, or how often, so long as you took your just deserts like a *macho*. He once made a consumptive boy finish his one hundred knee bends, although he had a note from his doctor excusing him from all physical activity. The boy collapsed on the floor and had to be taken by ambulance to a hospital. But he was back in school a month later and his parents, so far as I know, never complained.

My shyness soon gave me the reputation of class patsy. I

became fair game for any put-upon drudge driven to prove his "eggs" to his superiors by thrashing someone baser than himself.

In the third grade one afternoon I was challenged to fight by a Chinese boy, Carlos Huang, who called me a *maricón*—faggot. I accepted, of course, and a third party stepped in to arrange the time and place: the following noon in Miss McMillan's classroom.

My dominant reaction to the challenge was relief, not fear. Now the worst had come. I would get beaten up, my eyes would be blackened, and afterward perhaps they would leave me alone.

But a doubt lingered, and I consulted Father that night. My defeatist attitude angered Father, as I knew it would. He said the worst thing I could do was admit weakness to my enemies.

I protested, "But Carlos Huang is bigger than I," which was true. Though not much taller, he had a cushion of flab around the middle that would prove decisive in close combat.

"The important thing," said Father, "is to show resistance. If you stand your ground and fight back as well as you can—even if you get beaten—the others will respect you and will keep their distance. If you are weak and allow them to bully you, they will hound you again and again, and never give you a moment's peace." Then he added the clincher, against which there was no appeal: "Believe me, son, I speak from experience."

I resolved to take Father's advice, even if I got mauled.

When we met in the classroom the next day, the tension

was plain on Carlos's thick face; it was streaked with sweat. A girdle of dampness encircled his waist. I felt sorry for us both, two born scapegoats forced to turn on one another like Christians in a Roman spectacle.

My battle plan was simple. I would buffer Carlos's superior weight by refusing to wrestle. Instead, I would flail away at his face with both hands, until my strength gave out.

A self-appointed arbiter placed us in front of the room, against the blackboard. Roll was taken. The entire class was present. This was no ordinary schoolboy tussle.

"All right," the referee addressed me, stepping between us. "As the challenged you have the choice of styles. Wrestling, boxing, or free fight?"

"Free fight," I said. I looked straight into Carlos's eyes, as Father had instructed me to. Perspiration beaded his fat cheeks.

"Free fight then," said the referee. "I will give the signal."

A tiny bell tinkled. I shut my eyes and charged in, swinging blindly at Carlos's face.

It was all over in less than ten seconds. Out of at least two dozen roundhouse lefts and rights my fist found Carlos's face only once. The sensation was that of sinking one's knuckles in vulcanized rubber; it made no dent whatever. Carlos glanced a single blow off the top of my head, which inflicted no damage, except on Carlos's fist, which went on to collide with the blackboard. The cracking sound of bone on slate and the ensuing yelp of pain made me stop swinging and open my eyes. Carlos howled and hopped around the room with the injured hand between his thighs. The referee awarded me a technical victory in the first encounter.

For several weeks afterward I was treated with grudging respect by my classmates, just as Father had predicted.

A year later Carlos Huang, grown taller and thicker by several inches, challenged me to a rematch and bloodied my nose. But I wasn't called *maricón* again.

The Angel of Death

MY RESPECTABLE SHOWING in the fight with Carlos earned
me the attention of one of its promoters, a mestizo named
Eduardo Rodriguez. Eduardo's complexion was a lustrous
walnut. Against it were set intense black eyes with long
curling lashes that already won him special indulgences from
our female teachers.

From a distance I admired Eduardo's athletic grace and
skill (he was star center forward in soccer), his good looks,
and his winning ways with peers and adults. But there was
a hardness in him I shied from instinctively, even after he

made friendly overtures of a sort. Within my chambered self I felt his superior.

In the following weeks I was subjected by Eduardo to a series of tests. The first came during roll call one morning, soon after our promotion to fourth grade. We answered the roll in At Ease stance, our eyes forward, hands crossed behind.

Someone placed a moist object in my right palm. Reflexively I closed my hand around it. At the salute to the flag I snapped the hand to my temple and squinted for the duration of twelve stanzas of our national anthem at a clean-bitten green chili held inches from my right eye, between thumb and forefinger.

The chili was a highland variety that, had it brushed my eye, could have blinded it for weeks.

On another morning soon after this I walked into Miss Chavez's speech class to be greeted by an ominous hush. Miss Chavez was a soft-spoken, rather plain, impressionable young woman, fresh out of teachers' college. Our rowdiness was a trial she chose to endure unaided. She could have curbed us at any time by calling in Lieutenant Gonzalez, and we knew it; but her gallantry—we read it as weakness, a willing martyrdom—only spurred us on to worse abuses.

By the time I understood the charged silence of my classmates, it was too late. Miss Chavez had entered the room to find a message in one corner of the blackboard, written in Eduardo's unmistakable neat hand: "Miss Chavez *jode*" (Miss Chavez fucks). Below it was my name.

True to her code Miss Chavez did not report the incident to Lieutenant Gonzalez; had she done so, it would have meant my instant expulsion, and probably Eduardo's.

The third test was a duel. I reached inside my desk for

my notebook. Beside it I found a narrow glass tube, broken at one end, and a pile of tiny grains, a variety of millet used for chicken feed. An accompanying note read: "Outside the school at four-thirty. *Be there.*" It was signed The Angel of Death and sealed with a skull-and-crossbones. The tremor that shook my body was caused more by the challenger's signature than by his challenge. The Angel of Death seemed an apt epithet for Eduardo, though I wasn't sure why.

The glass tubes, lifted from a chemistry laboratory, made excellent blowguns. We used them during Carnival season to sting girls' legs or aimed them from the gallery at the array of bald heads in the front rows of movie theaters. The millet made deadly ammunition. Shaped like BBs, they were light enough so you could stuff a handful in your mouth and shoot them in rapid-fire bursts.

I kept my date with Eduardo. We drilled all the millet we had at each other until our faces, arms, and legs were swollen and red, as though from bee stings.

The next day Eduardo asked me to his grandparents' home for the weekend. To get Father's permission I lied and said Eduardo was the top-ranking student in the class.

Eduardo's family lived at the foot of a huge granite quarry, about eight kilometers south of the capital. He went there only on weekends; schooldays he stayed in the city with a cousin. To reach the quarry we had to take the number fourteen bus to the last stop and walk the remaining distance or hire a horse-drawn cab. We hadn't enough money for the hansom so we hiked the last three miles, which took up the better part of the afternoon. Along the way we got into a lively discussion, and the time passed pleasantly until Eduardo questioned me about being a Jew. Only when I felt certain his interest was genuine did I give straight answers to his queries. I had been through this catechism too many times before.

"And you truly don't believe in Christ, or the Virgin Mary?"

"No, but we believe in God, just as you do."

"Weren't you taught that Christ is God's Son, and his emissary on earth?"

"We believe Christ was only a man, like you and me. . . ."

Eduardo stopped, astonished.

"Of course, he was a good man," I hastily amended, "a *very* good man, much better than the rest of us"—Eduardo walked on mollified—"but we believe that God is One, and doesn't need emissaries on earth." But then I remembered Mother's incessant lament, "When oh when will the Messiah come and deliver us from Hitler?" and I wasn't so sure.

"Do you believe in the devil?"

I turned this one over. "Yes, we do. I think."

"Then why don't you believe that Christ is God's Son?"

"Because we don't, that's all. I don't know the exact reason. But we do believe in the coming of the Messiah, to save the world from Hitler."

"Who is the Messiah?"

"We won't know until he comes."

"Maybe Christ is the Messiah. Father Sánchez said there will be a Second Coming of Christ to save the world from wickedness and the devil."

"Yes, it could be. . . ." I balked at the idea, but could find no internal contradiction. "Maybe Christ and the Messiah *are* the same . . . Why not?" I thrilled at this sovereign deduction, which Father would have condemned as blasphemy.

I was doing my own thinking on a hallowed subject, and the effect was bracing.

Eduardo said, "That means Jews and Catholics are not so different after all."

"Perhaps not. Perhaps they're more alike than many people suppose." I dared further. "Perhaps they're even the same."

There was a long silence, which Eduardo ended by saying, "Be careful this evening. Father got drunk last week and said he was going to baptize you."

I stopped in my tracks. "*What?*"

He gave a mocking laugh, his black eyes flashing. "I'm only joking. Come on. We still have a kilometer to go, and it's growing dark."

Thick gray clouds had gathered overhead, creating a false dusk. We broke into a jog. The last houses were now behind us; only the rutted brown road and cow pasture stretched ahead. We passed an ox-cart whose driver dozed under a burlap sack, unmindful of the imminent downpour.

The granite quarry loomed tall above the plain, a jagged promontory menaced by the clouds. Suddenly the clouds parted. A stitch of lightning rent the quarry in half, but it healed at once. Then a loud clap.

"Through the fields, it's shorter!" Eduardo called, then vaulted a wire fence into the pasture. I climbed the fence after him, snagged my trouser cuff on the barbed wire, and fell on my face.

The first raindrops, though sparse, had the impact of aimed missiles. A hailstone struck my shoulder, and I knew we were in for it.

The skies opened as we zigzagged through a large herd of

browsing cows, as unconcerned by the storm as the cart-driver had been. Lightning flashed again, in the same instant that the word *bull* crossed my brain. I was seized by a terror so intense it wrenched the breath from my body, and I sank to my knees. Pelted by rain and hail I waited to be trampled and gored to death, or sundered in half by lightning. Through a seam in my terror the idea intruded that I had spoken blasphemy against God, and in retribution he was massing the forces of nature against me. But my mind rejected it. The storm was simply the storm, the bull—if there was one—was only itself; and I was in their way. I felt clear about this. My terror was pure.

Eduardo reached shelter far ahead of me. He and his grandfather raced across the pasture with ponchos, helped me to my feet, then half-dragged, half-carried me into the house.

At dinner, after a hot bath and a nap, I was presented to Eduardo's relations, all except Eduardo's father, who would not get in until late. He was a traveling agent for a plastics company and was on a tour of the coast. The Rodriguez family was far from affluent, but well-off by Guatemalan rural standards. They were part of a tiny but growing mestizo middle class. In one small two-bedroom house lived Eduardo's parents, his maternal grandparents, a young widowed aunt, and his four sisters, who ranged in age from a few months to eleven years.

I found these crowded living conditions a charming novelty. There was an intimacy here that I sorely missed in my own far roomier household. I liked most Eduardo's mother, Pilar, and her parents, Noño and Tonia, who were on a first-name basis with their grandchildren. My own grandparents, who lived in Palestine, were always referred to by their honorific or polite titles, which made them about as accessible as Rabbi Toledano or the white-bearded God of my nightmares.

Pilar was a small, very pretty woman, shockingly young to be the mother of five. Eduardo told me that she'd married at fifteen and had lost three children—one stillbirth, two to smallpox—before the eldest daughter was born. She was the fairest in the family and had Eduardo's luminous black eyes and long curling lashes, but without a trace of Eduardo's cruelty. Pilar seemed softer to me and more feminine, in a girlish way, than any woman I'd known. From the moment I was carried into the house, bone-chilled and in tears, she lavished so much care on me I became embarrassed and shied away from her.

Noño was foreman of the quarry, and the family's chief provider. His son-in-law's income from his travels was less dependable. He was a small, wiry man of about fifty, with a handsome walrus mustache. He rarely spoke, as if to do so in mixed company involved a diminution of patriarchal dignity to which he was unwilling to submit. Tonia by contrast was chatty and round and, like her daughter, Pilar, ceaselessly plied Eduardo and me with attentions. There wasn't a gray strand in her thick black tresses, which she tied with a white ribbon and draped over one shoulder, like a portly village wench.

For dinner Pilar made Eduardo's favorite dish, *chirmol*, a chili, onion, avocado, and tomato sauce so hot it cleared my sinuses just to sniff it. Its chief ingredient was the green *chilpepe* Eduardo had palmed on me for my first test. Tonia taught me to dilute the chili with rice and rolled tortilla so it didn't scald the tongue unbearably. After a few mouthfuls I grew so fond of the sauce I could not eat my fill.

When I passed the *chirmol* to Ana, the eldest daughter, she lifted a glance of appeal toward her mother, then shook her head.

"The *chirmol* is for the men," Pilar explained. "The women of the house eat something else."

Tonia gave a smiling grunt of endorsement to this and passed the bowl back to me.

"But why?" I said, refilling my plate. "It's not so hot."

"The men of the house are special." This was said by the aunt, Rosita. She underscored it with a wink that made my chili-flushed cheeks even warmer.

Rosita, like the others, looked absurdly young for an aunt, above all a widowed aunt. She was more like a flirtatious schoolgirl. I could not accustom myself to this eccentric, youthful family and their toy house. Noño and Tonia seemed not much older than my own parents. I wondered if Eduardo's father, too, was only a youth.

Pilar came round with the bowl and again filled my plate with *chirmol* and rice, despite my protestations.

There was nothing else to eat.

After dinner a cot was prepared for me. I was the only one in the house with a bed to himself. The three older sisters shared a mattress in the same room; Eduardo and his aunt slept on mats in the kitchen. The parents and grandparents were all in the other bedroom, with the baby sister.

I had just dropped to sleep, exhausted, when the slam of a screen door made me start awake. In this closeted house the least sound was magnified. The opening and closing of a screen door caused vibrations far beyond its importance. The entire house shook as boots tramped on the kitchen floor.

Curled snug under the blankets, I ordered myself to sleep.
"*Mamá yo quiero . . .*" sang a hoarse, booming voice.

> *Mamá yo quiero*
> *Mamá yo quiero una chupeta . . .*

I recognized the verses of a mildly obscene refrain: "Mother,
I want a lollipop."

A hollow bang on the adjoining wall, as of a lifted lid.
Rustling noises, heavy breathing.

(And still no possibility of sleep.)

A hissing torrent, followed by a series of unmistakable
farts, the first flatulent, then freighted ones.

> *Una chupeta*
> *Una chupeta*
> *Una chupeta para* unh unhh-ahhh
> *Ay ay ay Mamá yo quiero . . .*

Voiding sounds. Scraping. Silence. More scraping. Bang
of lid. I wait for the flush . . . then I remember. No flush.
House-shaking steps. More heavy breathing, rustling, the
groan of bedsprings.

(Still no sleep. I cannot will myself to sleep.)

"Less noise, Ernesto, you'll wake the boy."

Again bedsprings, louder than before.

"Aaaahaauummmnh chaeehmm . . . What boy?"

"Eduardo's friend. He's with the girls."

"Aaa, the Jew? Eduardo brought the little Jew from school?"

My heart stops.

"Quiet, Ernesto . . . *hombre.*"

"The little Jew from Eduardo's school, he's here?"

"Yes, he's here. Now let me sleep."

A muted slap.

"Ernesto, do me the grace to remove the hand. We cannot tonight."

"Of course we can tonight. The little Jew is here."

Another slap. A deep sigh.

"Ernesto, we cannot tonight. It's my night. I'm full of it tonight."

"Of course we can tonight."

The bedsprings grow insistent.

"Ernesto, beat me if you want. Anything you want, please, but not tonight. I am full of it tonight and it pains."

"Woman, of course tonight. I say tonight, yes. The little Jew is here and we will tonight so he can know in this house a man fucks his wife as God intended. Now turn yourself or I'll rip your asshole."

In the background of what followed, the grandfather's snores sounded regular and thick.

I slept late next morning. On waking, I prayed Eduardo's father would be gone from the house. But he sat at the breakfast table when I walked in, white shirt open at the neck, trouser suspenders down around the knees. My astonishment was brief, but complete; I wasn't sure if I concealed it from him. Eduardo's father was the darkest man I'd ever seen. His complexion was a polished rosewood to Eduardo's walnut and Pilar's blond maple. It didn't occur to me that he might be part Negro, chiefly because I had never seen a black man up close. Nearly all of Guatemala's blacks live on the Atlantic coast—West Indian Caribs hired by United Fruit to load banana boats.

We were formally introduced by Pilar, as if I were a rival suitor.

"*Mucho gusto*," I said, slipping my hand into his own huge one, where it vanished. Unlike the rest of the family he was a large man—a black Gulliver—and not nearly so youthful in appearance. He looked nearer Noño's age than Pilar's.

"*Encantado*," he said, and made a complimentary remark about Eduardo's choice of friends. He said he hoped I would help to educate Eduardo and make him civilized. A smile played on his handsome face as he spoke, which gave his words an ironic cast. It was the smile of a man who keeps his threats.

He did not address me again during breakfast, and I acted as casually as I was able under my burden of shame.

At noon Pilar packed a box lunch of black beans, rice, and coffee, which she asked Eduardo and me to take up to her father, atop the quarry.

As we trudged up the steep hillside Eduardo asked my opinion of his family.

"I like Pilar very much, and your grandparents. Your sisters seem all right too, but quiet."

Eduardo shrugged. "Sisters have no importance."

"Why, what do you mean?"

"They're weak. Too much trouble. Mother lost two girls before Ana was born. And they kept her only because she appeared strong."

I looked at Eduardo. "I don't understand . . ."

"Then clear out your ears, and listen." His eyes flashed. "The first two were permitted to die. It was not the smallpox. Father wasn't working then, and there wasn't much money. They would only have been two more mouths to feed."

I was appalled. "But that's—"

"Even now Noño pays for my education, which would not be possible if the girls had lived . . . Now you understand?"

I did not speak the words on my tongue. I asked instead, "And Ana? Doesn't she go to school?"

"A girl's place is in the house." Eduardo picked up a quartz fragment and chucked it at me. "Anyway, they're a nuisance. They don't really matter." He shagged another stone at my legs, which I leaped over. Then I tossed one at his foot without breaking stride.

In no time we were committed to all-out war. We picked our cover behind outcroppings in the rock-face and started throwing in earnest, small pieces at first, then bigger and heavier stones. I had a fair eye—though Eduardo threw farther—and kept him behind cover so he could not take careful aim. When the noon whistle blew Eduardo called a truce so we could get the lunch to Noño.

"How old is your aunt?" I asked, picking up where we'd left off.

"Twenty-one."

"What happened to her husband?"

"He was killed in an accident at the quarry two years ago."

"She seems—I don't know . . . coquette."

"She's been without a man too long." Eduardo smiled. "The other night she promised to teach me how it's done, as a present for my tenth birthday."

"She must be something," I said, masking panic. Suddenly I wished desperately to be home, among more familiar terrors.

"What did you think of my father?"

"He seems . . . proud," I said, after a moment.

"Did you hear him last night?"

"What? Hear what? What do you mean?"

Eduardo laughed, and I knew my face was red.

"Father says he baptized you last night."

೫೫

AUNT ROSITA KEPT her promise to Eduardo but waited a year longer, until his eleventh birthday. All that year Eduardo talked of nothing but *It*, of how great *It* was, and how many times he'd had *It* since his aunt broke him in. Against all inclination I had to feign a consuming interest in Eduardo's love life, and a readiness to rival it. Eduardo's resolve to initiate me became an obsession. He arranged trysts with a succession of shadowy "cousins" and "friends," none of which I kept. And yet I could not call an end to his goading and pandering by confessing disinterest. Our code did not allow for indifference to sex, at any age.

There was a painful scene on the school bus one afternoon when Eduardo persuaded a fifth-grade I.S. girl that I lusted after her and couldn't wait to get her alone in the park. The girl, who evidently was as precocious as Eduardo, darted me inflaming looks from the front of the bus. Far from feeling aroused I was repelled by her glances, by the acne that stippled her face, and by the unpleasant way her nostrils flared when she smiled.

Eduardo never went on to secondary school. His father died of cirrhosis of the liver before Eduardo was twelve, and all of Noño's income had to go into feeding and clothing the family, which now included another infant girl and a newborn male.

On my return from Guatemala after our first year in the States I found Eduardo working as messenger boy in a bank.

60

Five years later he was promoted to cashier. At eighteen he realized the prime mestizo ambition of knocking up the white boss's daughter.

There followed the Guatemalan equivalent of a shotgun wedding, from which Eduardo's style of life never recovered. Two years later, when I was a junior in Brooklyn College and manfully embarked on my first serious affair with a Barnard freshman, Coco wrote to say Eduardo was dead of leukemia.

I visited Eduardo's family the summer after his death. Pilar's greeting moved me to tears, in part from seeing her condition. Her small, graceful body had grown shapeless and slack, like a used envelope. Her face was bloated from extended mourning. She now had three grandchildren to look after, all by her eldest daughter, Ana, who was employed as a domestic in the city. The other girls worked in the quarry.

Noño's quiet dignity impressed me anew. He was the mainstay of the family still, at sixty-three. Of them all, the years had been kindest to Noño. His straight, wiry frame was untouched; only the walrus mustache had gone gray. Tonia had grown matronly thick, and her movements were deliberate, but she still wore her graying wench's braid over one shoulder.

Pilar fed me *chirmol* and the sweet bread I loved, as attentive to my whims as on my first visit. Then we reminisced. When I asked about Aunt Rosita there was silence. Tonia said she had gone off with a man and was living somewhere on the coast. She described the man, a traveling agent, as a wastrel and scoundrel who would bring ruin on Rosita.

"She deserves what she gets," Pilar said. "Rosita is no good."

With Eduardo's death the light had gone from their lives.

He had been their chief hope for rising above the curse of genteel poverty. But the period of grieving was almost over. Already the surviving male heir, Julito, was being groomed as Eduardo's successor. At age nine he had a bed all to himself, and he wore a spanking new white suit with long trousers. Julito had his mother's black eyes and long lashes. His father's hard glint was there too, when he laughed.

Before I left, Pilar asked me with earnest solicitude why at twenty-one I had not yet settled down to raise a family.

Doreen Dennis

LIEUTENANT GONZALEZ'S SADISM was matched by our abuse of foreign teachers.

Miss McMillan had given way, in the fourth grade, to one-eyed Miss Lind, who lasted exactly one hour; this was how long it took Gregorio Sánchez to build and set off a stink-bomb in the rear of the classroom. Her replacement was bandy-legged Miss McCoy from Glasgow, of the rolling r's: "Run Rrrobert run . . . rrrun to the railroad run. Rrrepeat after me, class. Rrrun Rrrobert run . . . . What is it, Francisco? What do you want *now*? *Can* you be excused? Ah, but the issue is not *can* you be excused, is it, Frrrancisco? The issue here is *may* you be excused, and the answer is No! Now kindly *sit down* and rrrepeat the exercises with the rest of the class, or I'll *chain* you to that desk myself. . . . Rrrun Rrrobert run. Rrrun to the railroad. . . . *What!* Who made that noise? I repeat, who was rrresponsible for that loud, rrrepellent sound? I will count to three. One . . . two . . ."

Miss McCoy grew suddenly homesick and returned to Scotland within a month.

Only Miss Gillead weathered, day after day, our war of attrition against vulnerable authority. She would not yield an inch to hooliganism, and held our respect with a rare blend of pluck and steely reserve. Her manner implied: Whatever you try, I have known and survived far worse.

We got a clue to her durability one afternoon when she told of an experience she'd had in London during the Blitz. One moment she and a close friend were running for shelter, after a late-sounding alarm. A shattering roar, and she came to on the ground, the wind knocked out of her but otherwise intact. Next to her the friend too lay untouched by the bomb, but dead. The explosion had sucked the air from her lungs and punctured them.

Miss Gillead's story affected me powerfully, partly because of my recent misadventure in the cow pasture. I rose straight from my seat and exclaimed, "Ghee wheez!"

Miss Gillead, astounded, laughed out loud for the first time in three years.

I was ragged and heckled for weeks after by my classmates, who nicknamed me *El Niño Ghee Wheez.*

None of our teachers was more systematically ill-used by

us than Miss Chavez, our homely native teacher of English speech, who replaced Miss McCoy.

It could be Miss Chavez somehow required rowdiness of us, as penance for her inadequacies as a teacher. And it's true she lacked a commanding presence. Addressing the class she exposed her flat chest and mousy soprano; facing the blackboard she gave away bow legs and a skinny rump. As if this were not damaging enough, her English accent was atrocious.

We could have forgiven the accent, her thin voice, even her chronic lack of preparation. Her cardinal sin was homeliness. We derived no joy, no real triumph, from imagining ourselves her masters.

Each day her supineness inspired us to new peaks of obscenity and abuse, until the afternoon we subjected Miss Chavez to the nearest thing to a gang-rape that nineteen aroused nine- and ten-year-olds can bring off. It began when Mateo Galvez, a large, mentally backward boy, was discovered masturbating in the rear of the room. Miss Chavez's audible gasp triggered a frenzy in the rest of the class.

Emboldened by exposure, Mateo climbed on a chair and leveled his erect penis at the rest of us, who could not boast his development.

"Miss Chavez *jode*," he shouted, quoting Eduardo's blackboard inscription of some weeks back.

At an esthetic distance from the scene, I noted that both Mateo's face and his penis were beet-purple.

"Miss Chavez *jode*." The cry was taken up. "Miss Chavez *jode*."

Three other boys climbed on their chairs and pulled out limp members.

"Miss Cha-vez *jode*. Miss Cha-vez *jode*. Miss Cha-vez *jode*." As one the entire class banged the phrase on desktops, in conga beat, as the four exposed boys danced on their seats, their penises aimed at Miss Chavez.

She was backed against the blackboard, one hand raised to stop herself from crying out, when Lieutenant Gonzalez walked in the door.

Mateo and the three others were expelled the next day. The rest of the class ran a hundred laps around the patio every afternoon for a month.

Miss Chavez's replacement for the final six weeks of the school term was Doreen Dennis of Dallas, Texas. Miss Dennis had sky-blue eyes, thick blond hair like threshed wheat. And she was close to six feet tall. No sooner had she spelled out her name on the blackboard in her inimitable calligraphy— fat, curly-topped D's, with vowels and consonants bunched behind like tidy ducklings—than we were helplessly hooked, every last one, on *La Triple-D*.

Doreen Dennis's impact on class discipline was galvanic. What three hundred hours of corporal punishment by Lieutenant Gonzalez had failed to impress on us, she accomplished with a gently drawled admonition, a light toss of her golden hair, a flash of her Colgate teeth.

No one was more smitten than Eduardo, who vowed to meet in the alleyway the first fourth-grader to show Miss Dennis disrespect.

My own infatuation verged on idolatry. I raised her to that exalted sisterhood of Hollywood goddesses and Wild West amazons who had begun to stalk and vamp through my daydreams.

Even our attitudes toward schoolwork changed. It was no

longer sissy to recite in front of the classroom, where one could better inhale Miss Dennis's dizzying fragrance. It became chic to pepper one's casual profanities with gringo slang: "*Ese* José *es un* dirty-double-crosser *cabrón*." "*Andá lamerme el culo*, son-of-a-bitch." "*La Triple-D si que tiene las chiches* well stacked, *verdá vos?*"

The boldest among us affected a Texas drawl.

Beneath our shaky truce fierce rivalries brewed over the momentous question "Which of us does *La Triple-D* favor above all the others?"

In the closing weeks each of us became separately persuaded, not only that he was the favored one, but that her choice would be crowned, at the opportune moment, with some delirious and unimagined reward.

On the final day of class, as was our custom, we delivered up our memory books to our teachers. In each of our books Doreen Dennis wrote: "It was really very nice of you to ask me to write in your book and quite a pleasure for me. Remember me, not only as a teacher, but also as a friend. As ever, Doreen Dennis." Under her signature she appended, "At home, Wednesday, June 3rd, 4:30 P.M.," and her address.

The entries were written in green ink.

🏵️

WE HARDLY KNEW one another out of khaki uniform. Punctually at four-thirty we all assembled at Doreen Dennis's doorstep, Sunday-suited, hair slicked, shoes polished to a mirror gleam. A buxom maid led us through the vestibule and into a sunny, carpeted living room, where we sat on wooden folding chairs of the kind rented out for wedding banquets. We waited in cathedral silence for our hostess to appear, assorted offerings balanced on our knees: dog-eared native orchids, bouquets of roses and carnations, cherry-centered chocolates.

At four forty-five Doreen Dennis made her entrance, spectacular in a flaring lavender skirt and matching sleeveless blouse, lavender lipstick, and spiked heels that lifted her margin over the tallest among us to a foot-and-a-half. Her blond hair fell casually over one cheek, like Veronica Lake's.

My heart thumped as she bent down to accept my bulging White Nun orchid in its chaste white box. She pecked my forehead in thanks and flashed her dazzling teeth. This formality was repeated eighteen times, with unvarying fidelity. She even thanked the class dunce, Gregorio Sánchez, who hadn't brought anything.

The maid appeared with sandwiches and a bowl of blood-red fruit punch, from which I sipped, wondering if it was laced.

Doreen Dennis then lined us up against the wall, shoulder to shoulder. She arranged the wooden chairs into a circle—all except one, which she folded and put aside. She turned on the victrola and played a Brazilian samba. I knew then this was *it*. Doreen Dennis was about to pick out her special favorite, singled out from all the others to be her dancing partner. I thrilled in the secret knowledge that I was that one. (Wasn't I first in line? Hadn't she kissed me first? Above all, wasn't I her top speller and irregular-verb conjugator?) But why then this sudden dread, this heaviness in my limbs as she explains in her mesmerizing Dallas drawl the significance of the folding-chair circle? One long white arm points to the victrola, the other points to the chairs, as she goes over the rules of this mysterious ceremony we must all submit to, before her choice is validated.

The test begins. I lead the march around the circle, dazed, uncertain, but determined to triumph, to vindicate Doreen Dennis's preference for me. The samba suddenly stops. Doreen Dennis shouts, "Everyone sit!" After a stunned instant, still uncertain but game, I drop into the nearest chair. Everyone else sits too. . . . But wait! Gregorio Sánchez, the class dunce, is left standing. Gregorio Sánchez, who neglected to bring a gift, and who is so dense he probably didn't understand the simple command, "Everyone sit," is without a seat of his own. Doreen Dennis pats Gregorio on the shoulder in consolation and signals him to a distant sofa, at the far end of the room. Then she folds and puts aside another chair.

The samba is played again. We go round the circle, warier now. Again the needle is abruptly lifted. This time Doreen Dennis merely gestures with her arms. I scramble for a seat ahead of the others. León Gutiérrez, the frog-eyed effeminate who pats rumps, is stranded and retires to the sofa. He is unworthy of Doreen Dennis. The design of this ritual is clearer now. It is a test of manliness. An old, familiar qualm rears its head, but I squash it.

She puts aside another chair and we go round the circle. The music stops. Fat Carlos Huang is squeezed out by tough little Joselito Yglesias, and has to join the two others on the sofa. Good! No one likes Carlos, my old adversary, who rides to school in a chauffeured limousine.

The contest grows grimmer. I am more alert now. I pick out my seat in advance, determined to pounce on it come what may.

Lorenzo Pérez, the tallest, handsomest boy in the class is

eliminated, along with studious and frail Gerardo Gutiérrez, who has the number one rank in the class. Arturo Sánchez, the class bully, drops out and is sent to the sofa despite his disgruntled protests. It now becomes clear that brains, good looks, brawn, and athletic prowess count for nothing in this contest. A less visible, more fundamental quality is being tried.

My confidence grows.

Finally only Eduardo and I are left, and between us a single folding chair. I have survived this far by a combination of wit and luck, but now my confidence wavers for the first time as I look across the chair into Eduardo's black eyes. At this moment our friendship means nothing to him. His eyes let me know that he is ready to die to win this test. I know then that I am not, and that he knows it.

The music starts and we circle each other like panthers in a cage. It strikes me at once that Doreen Dennis holds the outcome in her hand. Whoever is nearest the seat when she lifts the needle will automatically win.

She then does a curious thing. She begins to experiment with us. Her hand hovers over the victrola, moving to left and right like a snake's, testing our reflexes. Once she feints a break and we lunge for the chair, Eduardo winning. But the samba continues, loud, brassy, neutral, and we resume our prowling.

When she lifts the needle in earnest Eduardo and I are at exact poles from the seat. I pivot and slide in, but Eduardo has edged the chair toward him with his foot, and forces me out.

I do not contest his victory. It was foreordained. I can only console myself that she had made no clear choice between us, but left it to chance. I join the losers at the far end of the room, where we wait in silence for Eduardo to claim his prize. But Eduardo makes no move. Doreen Dennis shuts off the victrola and disappears inside the house. She returns with a tall blue paper hat, studded with silver spangles, which she places carefully on Eduardo's head. She bends down and pecks Eduardo on the just-visible center of his forehead.

"Now we shall play another interesting little game," she says, smiling at all of us, and disappears inside once more. She returns with a pink scarf and a hairy long object.

"This is called 'pin the tail on the donkey,' " she says, liltingly, enunciating each word, and blindfolds Eduardo with the pink scarf. She spins him around three times and places the hairy object in his hand.

High on the nearest wall her buxom maid has meantime tacked a square cloth with a red donkey crayoned on it. The donkey has no tail. I notice that the maid tacked it on briskly, without a wasted motion, as if she had done it before.

Miss Dennis also teaches the fifth and sixth grades.

Mar Abramowitz

SOON AFTER MY TENTH birthday Rabbi Toledano warned
Father that he had neglected my religious education, and said
I was in danger of growing up a godless heathen. Alarmed,
Father looked up from his ledgers and registers and saw that
Rabbi Toledano was right. His first-born and only son, three
short years from Bar Mitzvah, could not read a word of Scripture. This was hardly my fault. Our lingual tender at home
was a secular hash of native slang and Ladino Spanish: *"Manga
tu okra, ishto; 'scapa ya tus desmodres"* (Eat your okra, animal;

enough of your foolishness). Hebrew was for off-color jokes and adult secrets.

Father's alarm grew when he learned that his only male heir was a renegade who stole visits inside the cathedral, whose best friend was a mestizo goy of scant scholastic attainments—a male heir, furthermore, who gaped imbecilically when you quoted Talmud at him or asked him to recite the Commandments.

Father's first step was to teach me a Hebrew prayer that I was to repeat every night before retiring. The second was more drastic. After years of getting by as three-holiday Jews we began observing the Sabbath. At dusk on Friday evenings Father took me to the synagogue, where he tried to teach me my Aleph-Bet. But his patience was short and his mind would drift continually to business matters. If I did not pronounce the strange syllables perfectly on my second or third attempt he would snap his prayer shawl in my face, or slam the book shut, which instantly slammed my mind shut and turned my tongue to lead. After a half-dozen lessons I succeeded in memorizing the blessing to the Torah, which ends *"Baruch attah Adonai, noten hatorah"* (Blessed art Thou, oh Lord, who giveth the Torah). On the following Sabbath Rabbi Toledano called me to the altar and I recited the blessing before and after, pretending to read a passage from the scroll, moving my lips to Rabbi Toledano's words like a ventriloquist's dummy.

Father's lessons lasted only through Yom Kippur, after which the Christmas rush set in and he had to be in the store late on Friday evenings and all day on Saturdays. He gave up trying to teach me himself and engaged for my religious instruction a Polish war refugee, Mar Israel Abramowitz. Mar Abramowitz did not attend services in our temple. With a dozen or so other Ashkenazi refugees from Eastern Europe he worshiped in a tiny downtown loft that was said, by those who had never been inside it, to smell of rancid butter and pickled herring. Only on the High Holidays were the Poles and Litvaks allowed to defile our synagogue, and they had to sit toward the rear, next to the women.

Although I did not learn Hebrew for another two years, I was very early inculcated with the gospel of Sephardic caste. If all other Jews were Chosen, we were the Elect. We Sephardim were sole heirs to a remote but glorious Golden Age whose legacy we could batten on, without any effort on our part, until the Day of Judgment. At the end of the Golden Age we had nobly suffered the Inquisition, which resulted in our Expulsion from Spain and resettlement in a place called Diaspora. One day we would all reunite in the Promised Land, Eretz Israel, and begin an even more glorious second Golden Age, with God's blessing.

My earliest remembered "proof" of our legacy came at Yom Kippur. Toward the middle of the liturgy, before the blowing of the ram's horn that signaled God's presence among us, two men were summoned before the Ark: chinless, rail-thin Eliezer Cohen, a failure at business, and fat, famously henpecked Shlomo Kahan. Cohen and Kahan, whose names identified them as members of the priestly elite, first prayed in unison before the Ark. At a signal from Rabbi Toledano they draped their shawls over their homburgs and turned to the congregation, faceless. They were instantly transformed into hieratic mummers, impersonators of God's mystery, as they swayed from side to side with both arms raised, chanting His words in antiphonal responses.

Of course, it never occurred to me that Ashkenazim might have their own Cohens and Kahans to communicate God's blessing.

Mar Israel Abramowitz had been a successful lawyer in Warsaw before the Nazis came. Father said he had spent years in a concentration camp, but Mar Abramowitz did not talk of this and I never thought to ask him. I was not at all certain what a concentration camp was and had no special curiosity to find out. I knew only that it was a place where Jews suffered.

Suffering appeared to be Mar Abramowitz's chief occupation. He was a thick-set man in his middle fifties, with tufts of gray hair at either side of a squarish bald head. His bifocal glasses magnified a hollow look of grief in his eyes. His breath stank most of the time; nearly all his remaining teeth were black stumps. He had an ingrown right thumbnail, which he continually stroked. It was several sessions before I understood that the sighs and moans punctuating our lessons had no connection with me.

Mar Abramowitz managed to teach me enough Aleph-Bet so I could read a little Hebrew, but his suffering got the better of him before we could start on comprehension. I soon learned to take advantage of his infirmity. If his breath smelled especially rank and he stroked his nail more than usual, I knew I could get out of doing the drills and coax him into telling Bible stories instead. I liked these exotic tales, which Mar Abramowitz delivered with a heavy Slavic accent and his usual grieved expression. As he got into them, however, his

eyes would soften and he would grow almost eloquent, despite
his poor Spanish. The Old Testament stories seemed to ease
his suffering as much as they enhanced my tonic sense of
truancy from serious study.

In my youthful wisdom I knew they were mostly fables. I
lent no more real credence to a talking snake, the burning
bush, the parting of the Red Sea than I gave the prince who
turned into a frog, or to Billy Batson's instant metamorphosis
into Captain Marvel with the magical word Shazam. The fight-
ing and killing, on the other hand, I understood perfectly:
David and Goliath, Holofernes and Judith, the Canaanites
and the Babylonians, these made eminent sense. The battle
between the forces of good and the forces of evil, as I realized,
as Tarzan and Kit Carson and Buck Rogers and President
Roosevelt realized, was unending—and part of man's natural
estate.

There was a custom in our temple of auctioning off ritual
honors on the High Holidays. Rabbi Toledano or his sexton
would pace up and down the aisles, chanting the bids aloud
in Hebrew (while keeping the score on the fringes of his
shawl) so they sounded to my ears indistinguishable from the
liturgy: "I have thirty-five to open the Ark from Isaac Sultan
in praise of the Lord. . . . Forty . . . forty-five from Lázaro
Sabbaj in praise of the Lord. Shmuel Benchoam bids fifty
quetzalim to open the Ark in praise of the Lord, blessed be
His Name. . . ."

On Simchat Torah, in reward for the scant Hebrew phrases
Mar Abramowitz had dinned into my head, Father bought me
the bearing of the Scroll from the Ark to the Bimah. I crept
along the aisle with the red velvet Torah—junior size—hugged

to my chest as worshipers crowded around to kiss it. The Scroll was weighted down with a chased shield, chains, silver horns, and other ornaments, each separately bid for by the congregation. My fear of dropping the Torah and profaning Holy Scripture caused my feet to throb inside the corrective boots I wore for fallen arches.

My performance of this ceremonial honor evidently assuaged Father's conscience, for he never bought me another.

One week Mar Abramowitz did not show up for our lesson because, Mother said, he wasn't feeling well. (She used the Ladino *hazino* to dignify his unwellness.) But I guessed he was only suffering. I pictured him crouched in a corner of his room, breathing his foul breath, stroking his ingrown thumbnail, the grief-stricken eyes sunk deeper than ever in their sockets. He failed to come the following week and the week after that. When he finally appeared, I hardly recognized him. He had shrunk from a corpulent middle-aged man to a wizened gnome. The sag of his shoulders inside the loose-fitting jacket gave him the derelict look of a tramp. Only his sunken black eyes had life. The bifocals exaggerated what I recognized even then as the haunted, pinpoint gleam of madness.

Mar Abramowitz had come to excuse himself that he could no longer keep up my lessons because of his illness. His apology was rambling and disconnected and went on long after Mother assured him that she quite understood, and he was forgiven. Then, to my intense shame, Mar Abramowitz began to moan and cry aloud, right in our hallway, so that the sounds reverberated throughout the house. Mother fetched her handbag and placed in Mar Abramowitz's bony hand a folded bill. Brushing his eyes, he executed a courtly bow, pocketed the bill, and kissed Mother's hand before he shuffled out the door.

Three years later, on returning from the States, we learned that Mar Abramowitz had hanged himself.

The Prodigal Uncle

IN 1943 UNCLE MAIR returned to Guatemala from New York with his wife, Aunt Renee, and their two sons, seven-year-old Henry and three-year-old Michael. Like all the Nissen brothers Uncle Mair had put off marrying until his mid-thirties, when he was settled in life. He made up for his tardiness by choosing a statuesque Balkan Jewess, ten years younger than himself, who turned heads on Sexta Avenida and was a distinct social asset as well: Within a year of their arrival Aunt Renee was the most admired hostess in our community.

I had not seen Uncle Mair since my fifth birthday, when he presented me with an "Aztec gold" ring and took me to my first movie, *Snow White and the Seven Dwarfs*. I loved Snow White and became so frightened for her that Uncle Mair had to yank me out from under the seat and convince me it was all make-believe before I would unscrew my eyes.

The Aztec gold ring I lost in a silly contest with Coco Montcrassi, the gist of which was to see who could hop farthest with the ring clenched between his buttocks. I won the race, and lost the ring in high grass when I broke wind.

We spent an hour looking for that ring, under the pitchy doom that settles on a child's head when he thinks he has committed a fatal offense. Five years later my guilt was so keen over losing that worthless bauble (had I kept it, it would have turned green on my finger) I devised some excuse for not meeting Uncle Mair at the airport. I was sure he would ask first thing to see my little finger, like the witch in *Hansel and Gretel*.

My fears vanished the moment Uncle Mair walked in the door and shouted, "Here we are!" in a great booming voice, then lifted me up by the armpits and swung me around his head.

In the following weeks I studied Uncle Mair and Aunt Renee as a good acolyte studies his missal. I remembered Uncle Mair was hefty, but had conveniently forgotten that he towered above Father by six or seven inches. In high heels Aunt Renee was exactly as tall, which was an embarrassment not only to Father, who reached for his five-foot-five ceiling in her presence, but to Mother even more so, for beside her she inevitably looked like a plump and dowdy poor relation.

There were other troubling contrasts. Uncle Mair's appetite

totally outclassed Father's. If Father could wolf down a whole papaya at one sitting, Uncle Mair dispatched with no less relish a whole roast chicken! After his cyclopean dinners he stretched out on a sofa for his siesta; but first he propped both feet up on a hassock and systematically picked his teeth. Then he turned his pick around and scrabbled in his ears.

His trumpet snores could be heard from any part of the house.

In the genitalia match-up they were just about even (Uncle's longer, Father's thicker), but Uncle Mair pulled far ahead in the superhuman strength department. He had picture-book biceps that he toned every morning by tossing around a medicine ball—snap, heave, inhale, snap—forty or fifty times until his skin turned rubescent and sweat dripped from his handsome face. At midday he swam ten laps in the public baths.

Father had never taken time out for sports—the store consumed all his energies—so I knew it was important when I found him one morning on an old rowing exerciser he had hauled out of the garage.

Their behavior in the store provided another contrast. Father was staid and businesslike. He disliked haggling and always quoted the bottom price on principle. This unheard-of practice among merchants had given Father his reputation for probity.

Uncle Mair liked his chuckles. He would quote an outrageous price and jolly the customer along with ribald banter and repeated slaps on the back, making small concessions each time, until he convinced the client that he was getting a fantastic bargain. The sale would be clinched with a booming laugh and a last resounding whack, or, in the case of a woman, with a wink and a sly dig in the ribs. Uncle Mair frequently winked not only at clients, but at the salesgirls, and this did not seem to offend them.

About a month after Uncle Mair's arrival his bitter arguments with Father began. I would hear them from my room, shouting and banging fists on the table until late at night. When the house was finally quiet and I dozed off, a fresh round of shouting would start in the bedroom, between Father and Mother. One morning I got up the courage to ask Father what the shouting had been about. He said he and Uncle Mair were having a business discussion and I was to pay no attention.

If this was "discussion," what would a real argument be like? I pictured mangled bodies in the hallway.

Aunt Renee never argued or raised her voice, not even one time when Mother provoked her with a remark on her décolletage. Her manner was quiet persuasion and/or remonstrance. Whenever Aunt Renee appeared at the dinner table with a new dress or a costly ornament Mother accused her afterward of having "worked" on Uncle Mair to get it, since it was beyond their means. No one disputed this, least of all Aunt Renee. Uncle Mair was notoriously close with his money.

Aunt Renee had brought Becky and me coloring books from New York, among other, more elaborate presents. When Becky colored one trouser leg of a harlequin purple and the other green, Aunt Renee calmly shook her head.

"No, Rebecca, this will not do. People don't wear trouser legs of different colors."

"But it's a clown," Becky protested. "Clowns are different colors. . . . And this is *my* clown," she added, to which Aunt

Renee responded with cool, silent reproof. This was the first skirmish in the battle of wills that was to underscore their relationship all the following year, when Father and Mother went abroad and left us in her care.

My reaction to this incident was compounded of admiration for Becky's spunk and the abject admission that I would not have dared challenge Aunt Renee's authority. Lieutenant Gonzalez's discipline had left its mark.

Aunt Renee lost no time in becoming a pacesetter in fashion. She prevailed upon Uncle Mair to buy a car, a 1937 Packard coupe, which at wartime prices threatened the solvency, not only of Uncle Mair, but of the Nissen Brothers partnership. (Many of those nightlong "discussions" must have been over that extravagant coupe.) Aunt Renee drove the Packard down Sexta Avenida every evening to pick up Uncle Mair at the store. She was the first woman in Guatemala, Jewish or Gentile, to get behind the wheel of a car. And she was soon displaying herself at film premieres, at Saturday night poker parties, and at all Hadassah functions with a lighted cigarette in her hand, the first society matron to smoke in public.

Aunt Renee's "coups" are a matter of record. She was among the first in Guatemala to wear slacks, and perhaps the only one who carried off the shapeless numbers of that period with any style. After the war she was the first to import Parisian fashions and exhibit them in our synagogue, thereby starting the tradition of the High Holiday fashion competition. In her second year of membership Aunt Renee was elected president of the Hadassah Women's Zionist Organization, a post Mother had always coveted.

But she capped all her previous coups when she became

the first in the country to own a television set. She had brought it back from a trip to the States, in 1948, a full seventeen years before a TV relay station was set up in Guatemala City. I first saw the set, a ten-inch Du Mont, on our return from Brooklyn, where I had watched Uncle Milty on a fourteen-inch screen, so I was not unduly impressed. But Aunt Renee had a surprise in store, a remote-control switch that turned the set on and off from twenty paces.

The metaphysical nuance separating a lighted television screen with no picture from an unlighted television screen with no picture sufficed to provoke gasps of admiration from Aunt Renee's sisters in the Hadassah Bridge Club.

The Great Bookkeeping
Scandal

THE NIGHTLY QUARRELS BETWEEN Father and Uncle
Mair soon turned bitter and dangerously explosive. It was
clear they could no longer live under one roof. In January of
'45 my parents decided to go to New York for a year and
leave Becky and me with Aunt Renee. Father would buy yard
goods on Lower Broadway and ship them to Uncle Mair, who
would retail them in the store at three and four times their
wholesale value. If this proved workable, Father would send
for us at year's end and the arrangement would become permanent.

I did not feel acutely deprived by my parents' departure. At eleven I had outgrown Mother, and my attachment to Father had grown predominantly symbolic. It was Becky, barely eight at the time, who paid the price of separation. She was entering a vulnerable stage when adult support matters. In his fitful and distracted fashion Father had given Becky the affection she needed. Mother, however, slighted her unpardonably. I was her favorite, the repository of her thwarted longings and girlhood ambitions, which she persisted in living through me even as I edged farther away from her grasp. Mother hadn't the sense to conceal her bias from Becky. She was jealous of this fair-skinned, golden waif she had engendered, and she resented Father's open admiration for her. Only Becky could smooth the careworn ridges on Father's brow, however fleetingly, and make him forget his burdens.

I too was envious of Becky, and more than a little awed by her Nordic beauty. Mother and I were the swarthy ones. I begrudged Becky the pampering she got from Father's salesgirls and from our housemaids, who called her *canche* in the reverent tones the Mayas had accorded Cortez's blond, bearded captain, Pedro de Alvarado, even as he plundered their cities and temples. I didn't play much with Becky anymore. I had reached the age when it is considered *maricón* by one's peers to play jacks with your baby sister.

More and more, after Father and Mother went abroad, Becky was left to her own devices. I watched her grow distrustful, not only of Aunt Renee, but of all adults. She had no friends her own age and played strange, complicated games with her dolls. Late at night, long past her bedtime, I would overhear her conversations with an imaginary playmate who was half-human, half-cat.

Our *china*, Elvira, left us around this time to open a jewelry shop in Quezaltenango, so there was no one to comfort Becky the afternoon she had a ghastly experience of the sort only Elvira knew how to deal with. Becky bought a *tamal* from an Indian vendor on the cathedral steps and bit into a dead infant's finger. The three tiny joints, partially fleshed, had been mixed into the pork stuffing of the *tamal*. I could only stare in mute horror as Becky held the half-bitten finger in her hand, whimpering inconsolably. When I reported the incident to Aunt Renee her immediate response was to scold Becky for purchasing the unclean food. And she sent us both directly to bed with little Henry and the baby.

But Becky would not give in. Her stubborn will was the equal of Aunt Renee's. She did not yield an iota of her independence in the daily confrontations over bedtime hours and proper diet. The match was an uneven one, however; Aunt Renee had over Becky the incalculable advantages of age, size, authority. Finding no other outlet Becky turned her energies inward; she began to construct an insulated kingdom ruled by a nameless tyrant with inflexible will.

I managed to get along with Aunt Renee by submitting to her regimen, even when it meant not making an issue of boiled brussels sprouts or what friends I could bring home from school.

With Uncle Mair my relationship was more forthright. For close to a year I emulated slavishly his athletic example, which Father had failed to provide me. He took me swimming with little Henry three afternoons a week, and we tossed the medicine ball around half an hour each morning. Almost overnight I sprang a respectable pair of biceps. My calves filled. One by one I conquered my nagging physical disabilities. In six months I added a dozen pounds and two inches to my lanky frame, which edged me over five feet. That year I finally shed the orthopedic boots and went in for competitive sports, even soccer. A late bloomer, like all my male relatives, I was coming into boyhood a scant two years before— according to Jewish Law—I was to put it behind me forever.

Uncle Mair's example did not end with sports. He taught me to snap the towel after a swim so my skin tingled and glowed healthfully. (Mother used to wrap me in a terry-cloth tent and slowly rub me down, which left me feeling listless and vaguely debauched.) From Uncle Mair I acquired his laugh, an explosive staccato wholly disproportionate to my size, which I tried out on dogs and elderly ladies. He showed me how to use both ends of a toothpick, and how to grow my pinky fingernail long so it made a handy scrabbling tool for earwax. Uncle Mair introduced me to the unheralded, life-quickening properties of fresh radish juice.

It seems inevitable now that I should have turned against Uncle Mair eventually and sought out gentler models. Weeks before Father's return from New York I had ousted Uncle Mair from my pantheon. But I have not been able to shake off his influence as easily. To this day his idea of manliness goads me to compete in one tennis tournament after another, to seek membership in Polar Bear clubs, to roughhouse with nephews a fraction my age even when I would rather stretch out by the fire with a good book.

My reasons for deposing Uncle Mair were solid ones, and carefully researched. Foremost among them was a simple conflict of allegiance. As the arguments between Father and Uncle Mair grew increasingly sharp and divisive, the day neared when I would have to choose between them. Tradition required I side with Father, but a stubborn arbiter in me demanded evidence. There is no more unsparing judge of adult failings than a child with divided loyalties. During Father's absence I watched Uncle Mair's comings and goings like a hawk. I soon found squinting gaps in his armor. There was the Packard coupe, for a start. It was clear Aunt Renee had performed some jiggery-pokery to dislodge Uncle Mair from so much cash. Then there were the Parisian fashions, Aunt Renee's frequent trips to Mexico. . . . How could she afford all these luxuries unless there was truth to the report that she had a silken stranglehold on Uncle Mair and his purse strings? The verdict was inescapable: Uncle Mair was henpecked, a charge no one could level against Father.

Another flaw was Uncle Mair's embarrassing emotionalism. He broke into tears on the slightest pretext. I had often watched him at the cinema, which produced in Uncle Mair one of two unfailing responses: either he wept noisily or fell noisily asleep. Both reactions were about equally irritating to Aunt Renee and their closest neighbors.

Flamenco music turned him to a sentimental jelly because, he said, it recalled his Spanish origins and the suffering of his forebears during the Inquisition. Zionist speeches always wrenched tears from Uncle Mair's eyes, but he was not alone in this proclivity. Once every six months a fund-raiser for the Jewish National Fund would arrive from New York to deliver a breast-beating appeal for money, and the entire Sephardic community would slip its moorings and wash to sea on a flood of nostalgic largesse. With the exception of Aunt Renee, nothing could pry loose hard-earned dollars from Uncle Mair like the invocation of Zion.

"Im eshkakech Yerushalaim, tishkach yemini" (If I forget thee, O Jerusalem, may my right hand forget itself). This is the only Hebrew phrase Uncle Mair taught me, and it never fails to raise the short hairs on my neck. When I visited Jerusalem as a college student I heard from all my cousins and uncles and aunts that Uncle Mair alone, of all the prospering Nissens in the New World, remained obdurate to their pleas for clothing and money. It was the abstractions Zion and Eretz Israel that brought tears to Uncle Mair's eyes and loosened bills from his pockets. As for the hard-pressed, down-at-heel relatives who inhabit the abstraction, it was (and is) Uncle Mair's contention that they should better their lot with stronger initiative and hard work.

Not even Uncle Mair's courage was beyond question, as I discovered at dinner one afternoon when thunder rang suddenly out of a blue sky.

"Revolution!" Uncle Mair shouted, leaping to his feet. "Everyone calm!" His face turned waxen, and it retained that texture for several minutes after a second distant roll dispelled our alarm, and we all laughed. Uncle Mair had left for New York just before the October Revolution of 1944, and returned to Guatemala right after it, so he carried within him a full-blown phantom revolution all his own, liable to go off at any moment.

Uncle Mair's dishonesty was harder to swallow. I had overheard Father charge him, in the heat of argument, with bleeding more revenue from the business than was his due to gratify Aunt Renee's whims. While Father was away, incriminating evidence piled up. Aunt Renee bought a house in La Reforma, a fashionable suburb, that was easily twice the size of ours. She converted the vast drawing room into a gaming parlor that could accommodate her Hadassah Bridge Club on Thursday afternoons and Uncle Mair's Saturday night poker sessions with business cronies. I stayed up late one night while Aunt Renee was in Mexico and peered through a crack in my bedroom door at the red, blue, and white chips skimming like candy mints from one end of the green felt gaming tables to the other. (Years later I learned they were worth five, ten, and fifteen dollars apiece.) The clouds of cigar smoke drifting across the ceiling lights, the tinkle of ice cubes, the rolled-up sleeves and intent scowls, the bawdy-house repartee— they all gave Aunt Renee's parlor the atmosphere of a casino. This is the scene that is still conjured in my mind when I read in the newspapers of the smoke-filled room of a political convention or of the clandestine reunion of underworld bigwigs in some impeccably middle-class suburb.

Uncle Mair's management of the store grew slacker in proportion as he hiked the prices higher. And yet the business thrived. Father was sending him the latest designs from Dan River and Corn Hill, and in ever larger quantities. The demand they created among the fashion-conscious gentry in the capital permitted Uncle Mair to overprice criminally and still undercut his chief rivals, Mizrachi's El Casbah and Shlomo Kahan's Alejandria, for they did not have their own buyers in New York.

There was an appealing side to Uncle Mair's dishonesty that further strained my allegiances for a time. His easy ways with money—at least since the advent of Aunt Renee—made Father's compulsive thrift seem almost niggardly. However free and loose he may have played with Father's share of the profits, at least Uncle Mair derived some enjoyment from it. In the hot months, May and June, he closed the shop on Saturdays and Wednesday afternoons and spent them in the swimming pools or on expeditions to Antigua and the coast. I was with Uncle Mair the first time I saw the ocean, and it was he who took me on my first fishing trip, two large items on my balance sheet of loyalties. Father never found time for such idle pastimes.

The deathblow to my hero worship of Uncle Mair came right after Christmas, with the Great Bookkeeping Scandal. For months the suspicion had been building inside me that Uncle Mair, taken all in all, was obtuse. My suspicion was borne out the day the news broke that Don Pepe, our timid, mild-mannered Spanish bookkeeper, had absconded to San Salvador with ten thousand dollars of the Nissen brothers' capital funds. Ten thousand dollars is a large sum to bilk from a business with net assets of less than one hundred thousand, but Uncle Mair did not discover the defalcation until several days after meek Don Pepe had bolted. The bookkeeping scandal hit all the city newspapers, and circulated for months up and down the Jewish grapevine. It brought Father streaking back from New York in a rage. He spent weeks straightening out the books, all the while tongue-lashing Uncle Mair, who managed for once to look reasonably contrite.

My respect for Uncle Mair never fully recovered from this tailspin, but it would have waned in any event. The truth is, I had no more use for his example. I now found his posture on life shallow and hypocritical, and his hail-fellow tactics with customers downright repugnant.

Only when I saw a profound grief swallow Uncle Mair after

the violent death of his son Henry, did he resume in my adult eyes his former dimension.

⚏

IN 1948 WE moved to the States for good, and I did not see Uncle Mair and Aunt Renee again for five years. Father and Uncle Mair were as much at loggerheads as ever. Their second attempt at joint management of the store ended in bitter recriminations that opened between them an unhealable breach. In New York, Father became prey to the obsession that Uncle Mair schemed to wrest control of the business from him, with Aunt Renee's collusion. Three years later, at the age of fifty-three, Father suffered the stroke that killed the person in his body ten years before his death.

I was a freshman in Brooklyn College the day Uncle Mair and Aunt Renee appeared at the door of our apartment in Flatbush. I was alone. Becky was in a hospital on Long Island; my parents were in Israel on an extended convalescent stay. Uncle Mair had come to New York for a medical check-up, and Aunt Renee, as usual, to shop. (Since Father's stroke, Uncle Mair's covert hypochondria—the reverse coin of his medicine ball cult—had turned chronic.)

That Sunday I drove them to visit Becky in the private sanatorium to which Father had committed her after a policeman picked her up in Greenwich Village, half-naked, wandering around in a daze.

During the ride to the hospital Aunt Renee sat next to me without saying a word, her eyes on the road ahead. Whenever I accelerated to pass I could see her right foot rise from the floorboard. She always braked just ahead of me. On the expressway I drove faster and passed more cars than I normally dared to. Uncle Mair sprawled in the backseat, making predictable and contradictory remarks on the tragedy of Becky's illness, her wasted youth, the unncessary expense of a hospital when loving care from her mother and a healthful diet would straighten her out overnight.

We spoke first with Becky's doctor, an Austrian psychiatrist named Figelspiel whose grinding Teutonic heartiness gave me a faint vertigo. Uncle Mair asked the questions, most of them hygienic: Was Becky doing calisthenics? Did she eat a balanced diet? He was appalled that neither Doctor Figelspiel nor the ward superintendent had any knowledge of the therapeutic values of fresh radish juice.

Becky entered the waiting room, her faded blond hair in disarray, her eyes tiny and glazed behind swollen cheeks, one stocking bunched around her ankle. She was at least thirty pounds overweight. The color drained from Uncle Mair's face and he burst into tears. Aunt Renee smiled tentatively; then, when Becky made no response, she pursed her lips.

"You must take me out of here," Becky said to Uncle Mair. "My brother and my father are too weak to take me out, the radio controls them. . . . I don't like this place. Instead of a fish out of water, I feel like a fish in wine, or Coca-Cola." Uncle Mair hugged Becky and promised through his tears to do whatever he could. Becky and Aunt Renee exchanged only minimal courtesies all afternoon.

The next time I met Aunt Renee I had just returned to New York from a year of graduate study in Europe. Becky was back in a hospital after a brave but disastrous attempt to get through her sophomore year in college. Aunt Renee had come alone this time, not just to shop but to consult a pediatrician about her younger son's—Michael's—speech impediment.

She seemed remarkably mellowed. Over several cocktails and dinner at the Shanghai Dragon she confessed her weariness with the life of a fashion leader and social hostess. She said she liked nothing better now than to spend an afternoon at home with a good book. Her two sons, Henry, now nineteen, and Michael, fifteen, were a solace. "But," she added, "Mair is better at this than I am. He is like another man with his sons."

Aunt Renee did not inquire after Becky until we'd finished dinner and I had paid the check. I then told her all I knew about Becky's relapse. I said that on my return from Spain I had spoken with Becky's college counselor, who had warned that if Becky did not get immediate psychiatric help, she was likely to end up in the Hudson River. It had been several more months before I could persuade Father to pay for a private analyst for Becky. By then her depression had taken a deep hold and she had to be recommitted, to a state hospital this time as Father could no longer afford the private sanatorium.

"I have often felt," Aunt Renee said, "that I may have been harsh with Becky, in an effort to set high standards. I thought at the time that your mother was too lax with the two of you. But I see now that I was not ready for that responsibility. I had my own preoccupations. To be frank, I feel that I was no help to Becky."

Moved by this admission, I said that we had all failed Becky, each in our own way, but that this was not sufficient explanation for what was happening to her.

Aunt Renee nodded, and pursed her lips. I realized then this was her protection against tears, and it wasn't working.

�֍

I DID NOT learn of my great-grandfather's testament for another ten years, when I traveled to Israel on a journalistic assignment. Aunt Elsa, the eldest of my father's sisters, had sat me in her living room in Jerusalem and brought out the framed document, a family heirloom. Rachel, the youngest, translated it aloud as the three aunts peered intently over my shoulder.

In a flowing, prophetic Hebrew Rabbi Yitzhak Moshe Nissen admonished his sons and their descendants that they were not to leave the Holy Land without his consent, "from now until eternity."

"If ye have need to go abroad on a religious mission then ye shall go alone, and in no circumstances stay away from thine houses for more than six months.

"If ye heed my order not to live abroad from now until eternity, ye shall earn all the blessings of the Torah." Three are enumerated: Wealth, Honor, a Long Life.

The testament ends, "If ye comply with the above conditions then I, Yitzhak Moshe Nissen, Servant of God, forgive thee . . ."

"Your grandfather, Chaim, was the first to break the pledge," said Aunt Elsa, a stout, large-faced woman who barely came up to my shoulder. "He traveled to Alexandria in 1920 as a religious emissary. Two years later he died, and was buried on foreign soil. Shortly after that your father and brothers went to America. And look what happened to them."

The middle aunt, Smadar, who had worshiped Father, pointed

out that he had been considered the religious heir by the family, and had resisted his brothers' summons from Guatemala for five years, until their father, Chaim, died in Alexandria. She added placatingly, "But at least your father returned to the Holy Land to die, which is more than can be said for the others."

Aunt Elsa shook her head. "Your father, Isaac, was a stubborn man, like all the males in the family. They all refused to see the consequences of disobeying the testament and leaving holy soil." She clicked her tongue against her teeth, wagged one finger at me, and said nothing more. But I understood at last that the bitter quarrels between Father and Uncle Mair had far deeper roots than disagreements over the store and Aunt Renee's extravagances.

In 1971, after Henry was killed at age thirty-two in a freak boating accident on Guatemala's Pacific coast, a grief-dazed Uncle Mair had seen the workings of destiny, and of his grandfather's legacy.

"There are more things in this life," he had whispered to me with shining eyes, as we sat *shiva* for his first-born son, "than we can ever properly understand."

Only years after my father's death did I begin to see how deeply his guilt over leaving Jerusalem had infused the symbolic sacrifices he had acted out on his children, and on himself. In some recess of his weighted Talmudic conscience, he may even have been attempting to terminate the Nissen line, in the hope of placating his grandfather's ghost. Nevertheless, I still think of Father and Uncle Mair on occasion as having lived a parable from the Talmud, about the failed good brother who is forgiven in the end and the worldly one who gains fame and fortune, but forfeits his soul.

97

Since his death in 1961 my unresolved differences with Father have resurfaced in dreams, where they have taken on a whole new life. Some years ago I dreamed he gave me a gold fob watch, a family heirloom which he had withheld from me on my Bar Mitzvah. "Here—you're ready for it now," he conceded grudgingly, removing it from the folds of his seraphic robe and placing it in my hand. In a more recent dream he shouted at me, in the middle of a heated argument, "Look here—I may be dead, but I'm not senile!"

⁂

IN OCTOBER 1973, when I visited Mother in her small Tel Aviv apartment following the Yom Kippur War, I discovered that her thirty years in the New World had receded from her memory, like a dream of a previous existence. She had all but forgotten her Guatemalan vernacular and spoke almost exclusively in the Ladino of her girlhood.

When I took her in a taxi to visit Father's grave in Haifa, she looked at the clicking meter and burst out: *"Adió, esto mos va' costar lo que costó el higo de Adam harishon"* (My God, this trip will cost us what the fig cost Adam the first). Astounded, I remarked, "You mean apple, don't you, Mother? Adam ate an apple." She slapped the seat cushion with her open palm and insisted, "The saying is fig and fig it was!" Which, on reflection, makes good historical and botanical sense.

Mother is now eighty, and looks years older. She spends much of her time watching television and baking the Sephardic Middle Eastern dishes she loves: cheese and spinach *burrecas*, ground-meat *kubes*, and assorted marzipan and almond sweets. The '73 war had killed her favorite nephew,

Oded, a twenty-two-year-old army captain who died on a voluntary mission in Sinai. After listening to two Ladino radio programs and watching the late-night news on TV, Mother will sit for hours in the dark, sighing heavily.

"This war has had a bad effect on me," she says, staring at her gnarled hands. "Morally."

Fito

I MET ADOLFO RAMIREZ in Coco Montcrassi's house, the year before Uncle Mair arrived from New York. At that time I was living almost entirely in my private world, sustained by a dogged belief in my inner worth. Outwardly I was lazy and dyspeptic, a middling pupil in school, except in English. English was far more than a second language. It was my Open Sesame to the Promised Land of Limitless Possibility, just as lavish handouts to the Jewish National Fund were my parents' passport to *their* Zion.

Only a very few were admitted inside my sanctuary, and no one gained freer access than Fito Ramirez.

Fito was the son of the Montcrassis' cook, Doña Maria, a large, expansive mulatto who laughed with her whole body. Behind the laughter was a mordant humor that she clothed in proverbs. "What doesn't kill, fattens," she'd say, setting before me a hill of chilied tacos. When my cheeks flushed, and I gagged, I would first feel and then hear Doña Maria's rumbling laughter from the kitchen, like an approaching earthquake.

Although I shared one or two classes with Coco, and we visited in one another's homes, there was a strain on our friendship. Coco was a full grade above me and his marks, published in the honor roll each month, were like stellar points in a distant galaxy. These grades, and Coco's rapier wit, had confirmed his reputation as the school's first authentic prodigy.

It was not just his brains that distanced us, however, but his aristocratic pride. Coco was no longer the unassuming, curly-haired kid who had offered me his beret in kindergarten. In five years he had grown into an intellectual snob. I would not soon forget the afternoon he had put an end to Miss McMillan's harmless fables, which he endured from the back of the room with a look of dwindling forbearance. "Miss McMillain," he called out, in a lucid Académie Française accent, "I trust you weel not eencommode us with anothair nursery tale of thees eensipeed creature you call Feeshy-weeshy?"

"Why . . . why . . . of all the impertinence!" stammered Miss McMillan, stung right out of her fondness for deprived foreign children.

She returned to Indiana a disenchanted missionary.

Doña Maria laughed at Coco's pretensions and persisted in calling him Niño Coco, much to his annoyance. She knew how to take him down a peg with a well-aimed barb. "Crabs won't touch honey either," she'd say, if he made a sour face at one of her dishes; or, if he pestered her to be served quickly, "Patience, bedbug, the night is long." When he was more than ordinarily finicky with her food she would turn serious and remind him of the starving war orphans in France. In the end Coco would eat Doña Maria's cooking, but testily, his patrician conscience unmarked.

Doña Maria had been married to a traveling agent of Spanish and German descent, an alcoholic who one day deserted her and their only son and crossed the border into Mexico. Ten years later the circumstances of his desertion remained a fertile topic of speculation among domestics. Our own cook, Clara, was convinced that a seductive Indian maidservant, a Cobanera, had been the cause. For years Doña Maria supported herself and Fito with odd jobs as nanny, seamstress, and salesclerk in a department store. Although uneducated herself, a descendant of Quiché Indian farmers and Black Carib fishermen, she put Fito through private school; and she professed herself happier as a menial with a prominent family like the Montcrassis than she would be earning a comfortable living from less refined employers.

Fito was six or seven years older than Coco and me, but he was treated by the Montcrassis as Coco's coeval, if not his equal. A sensitive, virtual adult of seventeen, Fito resented the family's casual patronage and kept his distance from them all. He was especially wary of Coco, whose superior attitude grated on Fito by reminding him of his mixed ancestry.

When I first met Fito he had just been hired as a ground steward by Pan American Airways. He'd won the coveted job with his excellent American English, our shared love of which was the lasting mortar of our friendship. Our immediate bond was "The Hit Parade" and Frankie Sinatra.

The Civil Airport, where Fito worked, was a bustling, glamorous place in the forties. As a weekend attraction it easily outdrew the neighboring Aurora Zoo. I went there every other Sunday from Parque Central on the No. Five orange-and-blue bus, whose antiquated gears made every ride a bone-jarring adventure.

Over and above the unfailing thrill of a silver-and-blue Boeing Stratocruiser dropping from the skies like some shimmering, winged avatar and roaring gracefully down the runway, the airport offered an authentic Stateside canteen provisioned with malted milks, cheeseburgers, and, for the big spenders, two one-armed bandits direct from Las Vegas. Every now and then the airport staged a Hollywood spectacular, such as the afternoon the GIs landed.

I was in the large crowd of townspeople present when a fleet of B-36 transports arrived with several hundred troops to set up an army base at our airport. I watched breathlessly from the observation deck as the first flyspeck appeared on the horizon and swelled into a giant flying fortress. It made several passes over our heads, as if to verify our existence, before coasting to a three-point landing on the newly extended runway. A solemn hush fell over us, welcoming officials, plain oglers, and Gringophiles alike, as a tiny door in the plane's belly swung open and Joe Palooka leaped to the ground. He was followed by Clark Kent, Randolph Scott, Mickey Rooney, Archie Andrews, Donald O'Connor—all in their thin khaki disguises. Joe Palooka, the tallest of the lot, flung an olive duffel bag over one shoulder and waved a huge hand at us. "Aloha," he shouted, taking us all for Hawaiians, and covered the distance to the nearest building in six tremendous strides.

My faith in the Promised Land was vindicated that afternoon.

In this rarefied setting Fito Ramirez worked six days a week, the picture of jaunty confidence in his navy-blue uniform as he traded glib remarks with boarding and deplaning passengers:

"Yes, ma'am, Pan Am flight 602 is departing at seven-twenty-five, right on the button."

"Have you been checked through customs, sir? A mere formality, you understand, but it is required."

Sometimes his smooth, assured voice would crackle over the loudspeaker: "Attention, please. Pan American flight 136 to New Orleans has been delayed forty-five minutes due to technical difficulties. If you will kindly present your boarding passes at the canteen, a cocktail and a snack will be served to you, courtesy of Pan American. Thank you." Pause. "Attention, please. Pan American flight 136 to New Orleans has been delayed . . ."

I would loiter for hours around Fito's counter like a doting mother and eavesdrop on the tourists' reactions:

"My, what a *pleasant* young man," one globe-trotting grandmother would say to another. "Where do you suppose he learned such *nice* English?"

"Why from the gods, ma'am," I could have told her, "like

the rest of us True Believers. We learned it from Captain Marvel and Gary Cooper, Walt Disney and Sheena of the Jungle. Jiminy Crickets, ma'am, couldn't you tell? We've gone to school in that never-never land over the rainbow that spans from sea to shining sea, where the good guys always draw faster and drink milk instead of firewater; where they shout, 'Remember the Alamo!' 'The game's up, Nemesis!' 'Here's lead in your yellow belly!' as they zap all the bad guys from the halls of Montezuma to the shores of Tripoli. . . . Where the bad guys say, '*Achtung, Himmel!*' and 'Cheesit, the cops!' and 'I keel you, you dirty-double-crossing peeg'; where they shout 'Banzai!' when they mount an attack, and commit hara-kiri after they muff it—as inevitably they must. Where Crime Never Pays, but the Avenger's work is never done against the evil that lurks in the hearts of men. . . . Gee whillikins, ma'am," I might have said, "hadn't you *guessed?*"

The first time I brought Fito home he won over with his wit and dark good looks not only Mother, but Clara the cook and the maids of the exterior and the interior. Even Becky stayed to listen to Fito's stories, instead of playing with her dolls.

In the evening we tuned in "The Hit Parade" on our short-wave set and listened to Frankie sing, "Well, what do you know she smiled at me in my dreams last night" and "I'm gonna buy a paper doll that I can call my own." We knew these and the other eight hits of the week by heart, and hummed them along with Frankie and the girl vocalists. At the door, before we parted, Fito gave my backside an affectionate pat.

The following Saturday we went to a matinee triple-feature at the Palace: *The Hand of Fu Manchu*, a Gene Autry musical

western, and a Flash Gordon episode that ended with Buster
Crabbe and an Earth girl trapped between constricting walls.
Fito slipped his arm around my shoulder and I understood
he was the elder brother I had always yearned for, without
knowing it.

Fito came to see me at least once a week. He nearly always
brought something: a second-hand Tommy Dorsey record, a
back-date *National Geographic*, a rare stick of bubble gum
wangled from a tourist. After the GIs arrived to set up an
army base at our airport, Fito's job gave him access to the
PX, and he was soon bringing gifts for everyone—cotton
stockings and Johnson's First Aid cream for Clara, Hershey
bars, bobby pins for Micaela and Eulalia. For Mother he
brought, once a month, a carton of her favorite Camels. Fito
never came to the house without visiting the kitchen, where
he traded the latest gossip with Clara and twitted Micaela
and Eulalia about their *novios*. I usually waited outside; the
sounds from the kitchen were loud and cheerful, but there
was a dark undercurrent that made me feel an intruder.

Fito's visits left us in the best of spirits. Everyone loved
him. Becky laughed at his zany jokes and confided secrets
to him she would tell no one else. To me his visits became
a drug. I would wait for him by the doorstep on Sundays,
often as much as an hour before he was due.

But even Fito had enemies, as I learned the day I bragged
about him to Eduardo. He asked if I meant the Adolfo Ramirez
whose mother worked for the Montcrassis.

"Yes," I said.

Eduardo frowned. "Watch out for him. My father knew his
father before he ran away to Mexico. He was *hueco*, a queer.
And a German *hueco* at that, the worst kind. He kept boys

in all the towns on his route, very young boys of eight and nine that he paid to do things to him. They say he ran off to Mexico with another *hueco*, a boy our age." His eyes flashed. "*Hueco* fathers have *hueco* sons."

After the shock wore off, I dismissed the story as one of Eduardo's sex-induced morbid inventions. Since his seduction by his Aunt Rosita I had watched Eduardo grow more cunning and cynical. He was at odds not only with himself, but with me, for refusing to become a partner to his obsession.

Still, Eduardo planted a seed that I could not root out. The next time Fito patted my buttocks they tensed involuntarily, as if from a needle. I even questioned briefly if the squeezes and pinches he gave my biceps at the cinema were altogether brotherly squeezes and pinches. But these doubts passed, submerged by my feelings for Fito and by my need of him.

At the next Saturday matinee Fito's hand was palm-up on the seat when I sat down. I shifted instantly, and Fito withdrew the hand. I decided it had been an accident, but that night I had strange dreams, and for several nights following. In these dreams Eduardo and Fito wrestled on the ground, clutching one another by the throat. I knew it was me they were wrestling over. The next time Fito placed his hand on my seat I did not shift right away, and my conscience nagged me for days. Father had warned me never to sit in the balcony of the Palace because of the child molesters who lurked there. But my mind refused to make any connection between the faceless child molesters and Fito.

Besides, Fito and I sat in the orchestra.

As my dependency on Fito grew the twinges of conscience subsided and then vanished entirely. But not my dreams. By then Fito had gained complete acceptance in our household.

107

His welcome became official one Saturday when Mother asked him to stay to dinner. To my surprise Fito tried to beg off with more than just polite excuses, but he gave in after Mother and I insisted. In the afternoon we worked on a jigsaw puzzle he had brought from the PX, and later we tuned in "The Hit Parade." But Fito was not himself. He had a tic next to his left eyebrow, which tapped continually all after- noon. When he slipped into the kitchen, I overheard Clara chafing him for looking so glum. "Looks like the cockroaches got your tongue," she said.

Father arrived from the store late, as usual, and cross as a hungry bear. He did not address more than two words to Fito—or anyone else—during dinner, which he dispatched with some of the old élan. By contrast, Fito ate his food gingerly, as if wary of a bone lodging in his throat, though we were having shish kebab. I had never seen him so sub- dued.

After coffee and his laxative papaya, Father settled back with a sigh and loosened his belt.

"So you have been assisting my son with English?"

"Yes, sir," Fito said, in his snap-to-it ground-steward voice. "A little. But he already speaks it very well."

"Not as well as Fito," I said proudly.

"That is good. It is important you help my son with English. It is important that he speak it easily, conversationally. En- glish will be the lingua franca of the free world, after the war. There is no question about this. One will not be able to conduct business, or anything else, without good English."

"Yes, sir," Fito said, gravely attentive. "You're absolutely right." He had raised three fingers to his temple, to stop the tapping.

"Look at your mother and me," Father said, winking at us both. One of his rare expansive moods was coming on. "Between us we speak seven or eight languages: Hebrew, Arabic, German, Spanish, French, Italian, a little Russian, a smattering of Greek—and none of these mean very much in New York, because neither of us has a decent English."

"Habla for yourself, carbuncle," Mother said, in English and Ladino, and stuck out her tongue at Father. We all laughed.

The rest of the evening went splendidly. Fito's unease passed and the cockroaches gave back his tongue. He told hilarious anecdotes, did rollicking impersonations of the tourist types he had to contend with and their outlandish whims. Then the conversation turned serious. Father asked him about his future plans, and was visibly impressed with Fito's declared ambition (which was news to me) to be an interpreter one day at the United Nations—and this at a time when the UN was scarcely more than a blueprint. Fito had gauged correctly that Father was big on Roosevelt and large humanistic concepts like universal brotherhood and world order.

The high point of the evening was a story Fito told—or rather, performed—about two Jesuit priests. It held us all in thrall, trying to guess if there was a moral to the story or if it was only a joke.

"Two Jesuit fathers are strolling outside a cemetery wall at midnight, when they overhear a thin high voice on the other side: 'One for you, one for me. One for you, one for me . . .'

" 'Brother John, listen,' one of the Jesuit fathers says to the other, his face white as a sheet. 'It is the Devil and Our Lord dividing souls between them.'

"The second Jesuit father laughs out loud. 'Don't be a sap, Brother Peter, it is only two small boys swapping marbles or playing cards.'

" 'I tell you, Brother John, they are Satan and the All Powerful disguised as children, and they are dividing the souls between them.'

" 'One for you, one for me. One for you, one for me . . .'

" 'Don't be a pighead,' Brother John snaps, losing patience, but just then the voice at the other side stops, and there is silence . . ."

Fito looks around the dining room with a smile just below the surface of his dark, sensual face. He has caught us all in the web of his narrative, including the three eavesdroppers outside the door, Clara and the two maids. I exult in Fito's triumph and in the mastery he is exercising over all of us, even Father. If Fito can achieve this power with a simple *story*, what could he not accomplish if he *really* set his mind to it?

In his own voice, Fito explains, "As it happens, Brother Peter is partly right. Two boys have scaled the cemetery wall to steal apples from a tree. What Brother Peter does not even suspect is that two apples have fallen outside the wall, by their feet."

" 'Now let us go for the two outside,' says the thin voice at the other end, 'and split them between us.'

" 'All right,' answers a second high voice. 'Let's go.'

"The priests turn to one another in frozen terror. 'Brother Peter, forgive me, you were right—they *are* Satan and our Lord, and now they're coming after *us*!'

"The fathers crossed themselves and took off for the seminary at full tilt, their skirts flying in the wind . . ."

AT THE FOLLOWING Saturday matinee, when Fito placed his hand in my seat I did not flinch. After a while I did not mind the knuckly warmth under me, except when his fingers twitched. The bad dreams continued.

When Uncle Mair and Aunt Renee arrived from New York with their two sons, Fito stayed away from our house for weeks at a time. We met at the Palace for the Saturday matinees, as before, and Wednesdays I visited him at the airport. Fito never laid a hand on me while in uniform, and I respected him for this all the more. In any case our physical relationship had not gone beyond rump-patting and bicep-squeezing, which seemed a small price to pay for Fito's affection. But he would no longer come home with me, not even when I told him Mother had asked after him and wondered why he no longer had dinner with us. I did not mention that she missed her carton of Camels most of all.

My friendship with Fito faced its hardest test after my parents went abroad and we moved in with Uncle Mair and Aunt Renee, who had bought a sumptuous new home in La Reforma. Aunt Renee had heard of Fito and of his influence upon me, and she did not approve.

"Why don't you see more friends your own age?" she asked me at dinner one evening, her little sons Henry and Michael ogling the exchange as if it were an Olympic event. "What happened to the French boy?"

"Coco is in a higher grade," I said. "He's very busy."

"And Eduardo? Don't you see Eduardo? He seemed decent enough." By "decent" I guessed she meant presentable.

I shrugged. "He has other interests now."

"What kind of interests?" Uncle Mair's voice boomed from the far end of the vast dining table. He held a chicken drumstick partway to his mouth.

"He likes . . . women," I said.

I thought Uncle Mair would choke. "At *his* age?" He slammed his hand on the table. "That is a barbarity!" He took a savage bite of his drumstick, slapped it down, wiped his mouth. "I don't understand these people," he said, chewing furiously. "I don't understand this country. I don't understand this climate. It can all go to the devil."

Faintly smiling, Aunt Renee daubed her lips in the European manner, lightly.

"What's wrong with Jewish boys?" Uncle Mair shouted. He ripped off another piece of chicken leg, put it down on the plate. "Aren't there Jewish boys in your school?"

"Only one," I said. "Jacob Potorowski."

"Potorowski? The son of Jaime Potorowski? The Polack who sells cloth in the Chinese quarter?"

I nodded.

"Aaachhh." Uncle Mair waved his napkined hand, stuck the little finger of the other in his mouth, and scrabbled inside, so that his cheek balled up. He inspected the nail for residue, then wiped it once, twice on his napkin as one would a switchblade. "Better goyim than a Potorowski," he said.

My meetings with Fito became clandestine. Aunt Renee forbade me to attend the Saturday matinee by myself, so I took along Micaela and sometimes little Henry, now five, who had grown attached to me, and who loved Westerns. We sat together in the orchestra of the Palace, Fito in the center. When the lights went out Fito would slip his hand under my seat and whisper in Micaela's ear until she squirmed.

The more I came under the sway of Uncle Mair and Aunt Renee, the stronger my apprehension grew that there was something improper in my friendship with Fito. The seed Eduardo planted would not be quashed. One night I dreamed Uncle Mair, and not Eduardo, wrestled on the ground with Fito, as Aunt Renee looked on with a prim smile.

When Fito's exposure came, I was ready for it. We'd been seeing less and less of each other. Outside of our Saturday afternoon trysts at the Palace neither one sought the other out, as though by tacit agreement. I had stopped riding to the airport on Wednesdays; instead, I went swimming with Uncle Mair.

In some respects I had outgrown Fito. My English was now the equal of his, and I found Aunt Renee a worthier sparring partner. She spoke "cultured" American, a heady brew of *Vogue* and *Better Homes and Gardens*, to which she subscribed, and *The New Yorker*, which she read at her club.

At school Eduardo had finally aroused my interest in the opposite sex. It began unpromisingly at our fifth-grade Christmas party, to which were invited our counterparts in the girls' branch of the I.S. (The previous term Lieutenant Gonzalez's military tenure at the school had ended, reflecting the recent overthrow of General Jorge Ubico's thirteen-year dictatorship. The school was back on a civilian footing, under the urbane but firm directorship of a tweedy, pipe-smoking public school headmaster from Sussex, Mr. Albert Edmonton-Williams, who had an abiding faith in the civilizing influences of coeducation.)

The party was held in the fifth-grade classroom. A half-dozen of the latest sambas, rumbas, and tangos were stacked on the victrola and everyone got up to dance, except me. At first I could not believe my eyes, so stinging was my mortification. . . . Where had all these samba and tango wizards sprung from, all of a sudden? Had they *all* been practicing their one-two-threes and their shimmies while I loitered on Fito's effeminate hand at the Palace? Eduardo's smooth, hip-swinging style was especially provoking. He skimmed across the floor like a Valentino, clutching fast in his arms a fair-haired creature, taller than himself by a head, and with a more than technical premonition of rounded breasts. The urge stirred within me to challenge Eduardo for this prize.

Between records I cut in on Eduardo, as was the practice. We had not taken three steps together before my partner remarked aloud, looking down into my baffled countenance, "You can't dance." And, disengaging herself, she returned to her seat.

Humiliation spurred me to action. The next day Edna, Father's salesgirl, who was now a comely twenty-one, promised to coach me in the tango. I vowed to teach that tall, fair-haired, maddeningly desirable snob a lesson at the next party, which would be held at the girls' school on Three Kings' Day.

One afternoon that week Eduardo told Julia, the elderly cashier at the store, that he had seen Fito molesting little Henry in the orchestra of the Palace. Julia reported this to Uncle Mair, who telephoned Aunt Renee.

"I knew it," was Aunt Renee's reaction, as relayed by Micaela, who overheard her. "I knew it. I knew it. We will put a stop to this."

That night I was collected and cool under Uncle Mair's third degree. Aunt Renee made her presence felt without uttering a sound, just like in my dream. I assured Uncle Mair that Fito had not "assaulted" me or Henry, but was forced to concede the danger existed if the situation was not checked.

By the end of our "man to man" talk I had promised not only never to consort with Fito again, but to attack him physically the next time I saw him. A chemical change happened inside me as we plotted the ambush Eduardo and I would lay for Fito when he looked for me at school, so we could beat him up. During the last fifteen minutes of that session with Uncle Mair, and for forty-eight hours after it, I knew myself capable of a violent act against Fito, or anyone else. It was a novel and oddly cleansing experience. An added goad was my memory of Father's rebuke that I was too pampered and soft, and the world would trample on me. "I'll show him," I thought.

Fito did not try to see me again—alerted, I suspect, by Micaela, who had been dismissed by Aunt Renee—and my violent intentions toward him faded harmlessly in a few days. Before that I made my successful debut at the I.S. Three Kings' Day party. I danced three tangos with Eduardo's partner, her pubescent breasts pinned by my pointy shoulders.

By the time we went abroad I had all but forgotten Fito.

SOON AFTER MY return from the States the following summer, when I was thirteen, Eduardo and I were strolling down Sexta Avenida when he caught sight of Fito just ahead. In a mood for mischief, we crept up behind him. But something was wrong. Fito was not the kind you crept up on so easily. Among his talents was a remarkable faculty for catching sight of you first, *always*, with one brow raised and a wry smile just under the surface of his face. This hawk-eye was a survival mechanism, and it wasn't functioning. His gait, too, was all wrong. As we passed on either side of him Eduardo muttered an obscenity in his ear. I turned, and the taunt died on my lips. His face was a painted mask. Everything I knew of Fito's features was gouged out, covered over with a dusting of powder and a daub of rouge. We passed without exchanging recognition. I'm not even certain that he saw me.

That night Eduardo told me that Fito had been fired from his job after he was discovered having homosexual relations with another ground steward. He could not find work and soon became a notorious prostitute, a *puto* who made his living from lonely GIs and foreign queers.

"Had you really seen him with Henry and Micaela in the orchestra of the Palace?" I asked Eduardo, and he admitted finally that he had not, but had been told by a friend of his whom Fito had tried to pick up.

"Anyway, it doesn't matter if I saw him or not," Eduardo said. "I knew he would try it sooner or later." His eyes flashed. "*Huecos* are all alike. They are just a nuisance. If I were president, I would castrate all of them, every last one, and throw them in jail."

Jorge Ubico

THE PRESIDENCY OF GENERAL Jorge Ubico spanned the first ten years of my life. As I was growing up he came to represent not only fatherly *caudillo* and Lord of the Manor, but quite literally the Man on the White Horse: Once a year, on his birthday, he paraded the length of Sexta Avenida on a magnificent prancing stallion. The rest of the time he was the ubiquitous but unseen Presence, manifest in the snap of the Honor Guard's boots as they marched past the National Palace, in the whipped faces of the Indians who swept the city's streets, and in the slouch and shuffle of chain-ganged convicts who built the country's roads. I felt his presence most intimately in the mammoth gray eminence, his cousin *La Maciste*, as she strode mannishly up and down Parque Central during her morning constitutional.

In November 1938, when I was not yet five, President Ubico commemorated the seventh anniversary of his rule with a *Feria Nacional* that was to rival in everything but size the World's Fair in New York. I was taken to the fair by pretty Edna, who had just turned sixteen and was wearing lipstick and silk stockings for the first time. The jasmine scent she had sprayed on herself imparts a sickly sweet redolence to my memories of that day.

The fairground, on a level plateau south of the capital, was dominated by a giant roller coaster, "the Russian Mountain," which still stands today, rusted and useless, in the middle of a squatters' colony. I could not look at the cars plunging down its slopes without my legs going queer; no one, certainly not Edna, could convince me the screaming people trapped inside the cars were having fun.

It was easier to look at the red and blue cars that skidded and bumped head on, shooting off sparks, or at the enormous boots on long stilts that swung end over end, faster and faster, with more screaming people inside them. Edna called this Loopdeloop, and she said this was all right too, because the people were enjoying themselves. But I made her wait for them to come out.

These mechanical diversions were only a part of the fair's fascination. There were gentler novelties like pink sugar puffs, bigger than Edna's head, that melted in your mouth so you could eat it all and not get stuffed. There was a pavilion where you won a prize if the man with the tumbling basket called out all the pictures on your card, like a crown, a peacock, a grinning death's-head.

The most interesting place in all the fair was a large area encircled by a tall bamboo fence. In one corner of this enclosure, behind a smaller fence guarded by soldiers, a group of Lacandones lived in huts of bamboo and thatch. The men on display wore dirty white shifts, and they had lighter skins than the Indians I saw in the street—lighter even than *El Sincarne*, the crippled beggar Elvira had said was a Lacandon. Like *El Sincarne*'s the hair of the Lacandones grew down to their shoulders, so you could not be certain of their sex. But unlike *El Sincarne*, whose hair was straight and smooth, their hair was thickly matted, as if it had never been combed. Edna said they rubbed ox-dung on their hair, which is why it was so unruly; but she smiled when she said this, so I took it to be a joke. All the Lacandones walked in a half-crouch, as if the roofs of their huts were too low. One of the men came out of his hut and walked right to the place at the fence where we stood. He looked down at me with sad, beautiful eyes and made a noise in his throat. "Tennh," he said again, and stuck his hand through a hole in the fence like the chimpanzee in the zoo. But a soldier pulled him away before I could decide whether to give him a coin or a stale chocolate in my trouser pocket, as my heart thumped against my ribs.

Outside one of the huts a woman weaved on a loom a beautiful cloth with bands of bright colors running across it. Edna said she was just an ordinary Indian from Sololá, not a Lacandona. She said the Lacandones were as old as the Maya, who had lived in Guatemala many years before the Spanish arrived.

"Are you an Indian, Edna?" I had noticed her wide, flat

nose and high cheeks were like the weaving woman's, though her skin wasn't as brown.

"I am mestiza."

"What is mestiza?"

She thought a moment, biting her lipsticked underlip. "Mestiza is like *café con leche.* Coffee with milk."

At the other end of the enclosure was an enormous tall pole with a small round platform at the top. Four Indians in red headdress shinnied up to the swinging platform and tied ropes around their waists, while a fifth sat on the turning capstan and played a flute. Then they jumped free of the platform, upside down. They swung around and around the pole without bumping one another, lower and lower until their heads grazed the ground. At the last moment they jerked upright and landed on their feet, running.

For all of these wonders I felt personally indebted to our president, General Jorge Ubico. Who else but an all-powerful ruler could command such spectacles for his anniversary?

It was several more years before I came to grips with the sinister underside of Ubico's paternalistic rule. Most infamous of all his tyrannical decrees was his *Ley de Fuga.* Under this unwritten law thieves, "communists," political rivals, hostile journalists were picked up without warrants by the National Police. After "interrogation" in police headquarters they were set free in a pasture, more dead than alive, and shot in the back, "attempting to flee."

"I am like Hitler," Ubico boasted once. "I execute first and give trial afterward."

General Ubico was forced out of office in July 1944 by a coalition movement led by lawyers and university students. Faced with growing civil opposition and the humiliating prospect of a mutiny within his military, Ubico entrusted the government to a handpicked triumvirate of colonels and left the country in a colossal sulk, with much of its treasury. He set up camp in New Orleans, where he lived in the accustomed style of rich, exiled benevolent despots who bide their time. But the awaited summons never came. The revolution had only begun, and his former subjects were happily rid of him.

Two years after his ouster Ubico was dead, reportedly of a broken heart.

Federico Ponce

IN THE MONTHS FOLLOWING Ubico's overthrow the revolution gathered momentum. The discontent in the capital was exacerbated by the abuses of Ubico's provisional successor, Colonel Federico Ponce, who, it was said, cast himself in Ubico's image and threw away the mold. Early in his term he invaded the Congress in an attempt to circumvent elections and perpetuate himself in office. He rounded up the heads of opposition parties and tossed them summarily behind bars as "communists" and "anarchists." Reports soon spread that Federico Ponce had assassinated more enemies—including the editor of an independent newspaper—and extorted more money from the treasury during his three months in office than had his predecessor in thirteen years.

University students again were the vanguard of the opposition. The more militant formed a party with a vague Marxist orientation, El Frente Libertador Popular (The Popular Liberation Front). Among the thousands taking part in the two activities of the day—*huelga y manifestación* (strike and mass demonstration)—was my relative Jacob, a freshman in the medical school of San Carlos University. I saw Jacob once, marching arm-in-arm down Sexta Avenida with dozens of smooth-cheeked revolutionaries like himself. They chanted an anti-Ponce lampoon:

> *Quisiera tener la suerte*
> *La suerte de 'Lico Ponce*
> *Que tiene dieciocho hijos*
> *Y a ninguno los mantiene.*

> I wish I had the luck
> of 'Lico Ponce
> Who has eighteen sons
> And doesn't support even one.

The verses parodied a popular refrain about a single rooster in his henyard.

The Pick-Up

'LICO PONCE AND HIS EIGHTEEN sons, *El Sincarne*, *La Maciste*—and, later on, the Brothers Bush—these were the real stuff of legend, which I rejected in favor of Hollywood and its roving emissaries, the American GIs.

From Father's store I spied on these paragons as they prowled Sexta Avenida in the loose-limbed, shambling gait peculiar to their kind. Grown bolder I stalked them in the streets to learn their haunts, in readiness for the day when I would single out one among them and confide to him my true identity. We would then become friends for life. At the movies

I sat behind them and exclaimed, "Oh boy" and "Jeepers" at the witty lines, just ahead of the Spanish subtitles. I grew bolder still and sat next to a likely candidate on the bus, but the alcohol on his breath drove me off before I could broach our common interests. Another GI wandered into the store to inquire if we sold native cloth. I directed him to the marketplace in John Wayne American. He thanked me in Berlitz Spanish and shuffled away.

The big break came unexpectedly one afternoon on my way home from school. Crossing Parque Central I came upon a lone GI seated by the fountain next to the labyrinth. He gazed intently at the goldfish cruising near the bottom. I ducked behind a pillar and sized up my quarry. He was smaller than the general run of GIs, about 5'7", and had a runty face, outsize ears, and very prominent buck teeth. But there was something winning in the religious absorption of his red little eyes in those goldfish. My values at this time favored leanness and spirituality. My GI had both of these and something else besides, equally appealing. He looked vulnerable and in urgent need of a friend. A man of such qualities, I reasoned, must lead a rich inner life.

I made my move.

"Hi, solgher. Got the tahm?"

"Whazzat!" The GI leaped up from the fountain and nearly fell in.

"The tahm," I said, in my John Wayne drawl. "Do you got the keerect tahm?"

"Oh yeah. Sure. Four-forty-five. . . . Geez, kid, you shouldn't of done that. I almost fell in." He squinted at my shoulder-strap schoolbag, my khaki shorts, shirt, and tie. "You American?"

125

"Sure, Yank. I'm Central American."

He pushed back his cap, raised both hands to his waist. "What I mean is, are you from the States?"

I straightened up. "No, but I hope to arrive there one day."

"I'll be damned." Squinting at me so that his teeth jutted out more than ever, he hitched up his trousers, sat down by the fountain, and rubbed the back of his cropped head. "Where'd ya learn English? It's pretty good."

"At the International School," I said, transfixed by his teeth.

"You don't say so. I'll be damned. Must be a pretty good school." Again he squinted at me. "How old are ya, anyway? Nine?"

"Ten-and-a-half." Pride competed with shame about my size. But he wasn't that much bigger.

"You don't say. That's pretty good for ten-and-a-half."

He chomped distractedly on a ball of gum, slapped his thigh again for no apparent reason. I saw he had braces on those upper front teeth, which crowded out the gentler features on his small face.

He signaled to me with one finger. "Say, lissen, kid, you know this town, right? You were born here?"

I nodded.

"You know a place in this town I can buy an egg cream?"

I stared at him. "Egg cream?"

He sighed. "Well, never mind egg cream. Skip the egg cream. Where can I get a milkshake, or a cherry malted?"

Illumination. "Oh sure. At Jensen's. They have as well hamburgers. I'll accompany you personally."

On the way to Jensen's, Murray Schaatz, p.f.c., as he identified himself, asked me how a ten-year-old kid could learn English so good. I told him about Miss Gillead and Doreen Dennis, about the books I read and the movies I went to. I asked where he was from and he said Coney Island, Brooklyn. I nodded smartly. I knew of Coney Island from a postcard Aunt Margo had sent us. Murray said he was twenty-two years old and had worked as a movie usher and a sideshow barker before he was drafted. I asked what a sideshow barker was, and he replied with a string of obscure synonyms.

"A spieler, you know, a pitchman; the guy who stands outside and ballyhoos . . ."

"Ballyhoos?"

"Sure, the guy who talks up the show, brings out a pair of hoofers to draw the marks in."

I asked Murray what was inside the sideshow.

"Freaks. Strippers. Ringers. The alligator girl. Tirza the wine-bath girl." He squinted at me. "The mule-faced boy. Sword-swallowers . . . like that. Of course most of them are phonies. Take the alligator girl, Wanda Borowski. She was a nice Polish kid with a skin disease. She had these ugly scabs all over her body. A nice kid, though, lost her family in the war. I took her out a couple of times. You know, dancing . . ." He mimicked a rumba with his shoulders and hips.

I envisioned Murray clutching a girl-faced creature with green scales running the length of its body to the tip of a thick, pointed tail. Where, I wondered, did one take an alligator girl dancing? But I didn't dare ask Murray. I asked instead, "What about the mule-faced boy, Murray?"

"Oh, he was just a poor sap with big ears and buck teeth. . . . Then there was Robert-Roberta, half-man, half-woman." Murray laughed, sucked his underlip. "She was a real card. Her voice was deep as a man's, which spooked a lot of people, and she had surgery done on one of her tits." He illustrated the process with a slice of his hand. "Roberta had a lot of hair on her face, arms, and legs, and she shaved off one side of it every day." Murray sniggered, looked sidewise at me. "It cost two bits extra to go backstage and peek at her pussy."

"Pussy?"

"Pussy, you know—her private parts."

"Oh," I said, and then uncertainly, "how many did she have, Murray?"

Murray roared. "Hymie, you're a good kid," he said, and slapped my back.

At Jensen's Murray ordered a cherry malted and a hamburger for himself and a vanilla shake for me. When he'd finished he drank two glasses of water and burped a few times.

"Lissen, Hymie"—he leaned close to whisper in my ear—"where can I get me a good-looking dame in this town? You know, for dancing?" He did his puppet rumba with his shoulders.

I thought hard, but could not think of anybody. I said I would ask around and let him know the next day.

"Fine," Murray said. "Just fine, Hymie. You're a good kid. I want you to know I really appreciate this." He fished out a Hershey bar from his shirt pocket and pressed it into my hand, as if it were a priceless amulet. In Murray's eyes was the intensely spiritual gaze he had leveled on the goldfish. I knew now what that gaze meant. It meant Murray was myopic.

We agreed to meet by the fountain the following afternoon.

I talked to Eduardo the next morning, and he gave me the address of a dance-parlor on Quinta Avenida. Eduardo claimed he patronized the place once a week, "and not for dancing alone," but I knew he couldn't afford it.

I waited for Murray by the fountain all afternoon. He never showed up.

A few days later I saw Murray strolling down Sexta Avenida. I shadowed him a few blocks, but he seemed to have no special destination. He would peer vacantly into shop windows, jingle coins in his trouser pockets, fidget with his cap. At one intersection he stopped to squint absently into space, with hands on hips. Murray Schaatz was homesick and in need of a friend.

I crossed the street and slowed to a crawl, pretending not to have seen him.

"Hey, you—kid."

I spun around. "Oh hi, Murray."

"Hi, there—er—Howie."

"Jaime."

"What?"

"My name is Jaime, Jimmy."

"Oh sure, I *meant* Hymie. Lissen." He bent over, passed his tongue over his braces. "I'm sorry I didn't show last week. I got held up at the base, O.K.?"

"O.K.," I said, believing, instantly forgiving.

"Did you ask around about—you know"—he went through his rumba wiggles—"what I mentioned the other day?"

"Yes," I said. "I can take you now, if you want."

"On the level? Howie, you're a real good kid, you know that?"

"Jaime."

"I *meant* Hymie. . . . Where is she?"

"Come." I led Murray to Quinta Avenida, then five blocks south past Parque Concordia and the Chinese quarter, until we came to a canteen with a red tin rooster above the entrance. The neon marquee read El Gallo. I pushed open the adjoining door, which led to a steep, narrow stairway with a blinking red light at the top.

Shrill female voices filtered down.

Murray peered inside the door and turned away, shaking his head. "Uh uh. This isn't what I had in mind. I want a *nice* dame, you understand? A senhoreeta I can take dancing at the base, not one of these lousy tramps. You know what I mean, dancing?" Again he mimed the rumba. "Dancing. No fuckee fuckee. I'm not interested in that now. I *had* that in Honolulu. No likee likee now. Lissen, Hymie, she doesn't have to be a knockout. Just a nice, friendly homebody girl, you understand? Hey, I got it." He snapped his fingers and bent down close to my face. "Didn't you say your old man worked in a shoestore or something?"

I nodded, not bothering to remind him it was a textiles store, which Father owned.

"Well, there are women working there, right? Some nice young salesgirl who'll go dancing with me?"

I pictured Murray dancing with Edna, who had shapely legs and was not yet twenty-one, or with Marina, who was older but had big motherly breasts. Marina, I suspected, would not turn down an invitation from an American soldier, not even Murray. But the idea was repugnant. Edna and Marina, they were Father's employees, which meant I had a small stake in them too. And, in a way, I had a stake in Murray. A little bit of him belonged to me. I shrank from mixing up my investments in this way, jeopardizing both.

"No, Murray," I said.

Murray sighed, straightened up. "Look, Hymie boy, I thought we were buddies." A change came over his face that made my stomach contract. I wanted to reach out and explain to Murray, but I was prevented by a sinking dread. He squinted at me, sucked his underlip with his grotesque teeth. "Lissen," he said, in a calmer tone I instantly distrusted, "I've got two Hershey bars in my pocket. They're yours. And I've got plenty more at the base." He bent down, pushed back his cap. "I've also got American cigarettes. You can sell Lucky Strikes in the black market for fifty centavos a pack." He tried to wedge the chocolate bars into my hand, but I held back.

"No, Murray."

Again he sighed. He hitched up his trousers, passed his tongue over his braces. At that moment I guessed Murray's secret. He was the mule-faced boy in the sideshow.

"Hymie, I thought you were different. I thought we were pals. . . ." He jingled coins in his pocket. "Is it baksheesh you want?"

I shook my head.

"Stop playing coy, for Chrissake!" Murray's face hardened. "Look, you don't have to put up this front, see? There are dozens of kids no better than you that are on my tail all the time to take out their sisters. . . . Dozens, see? All I have to do is snap my fingers—like that—and hundreds of runny-nosed brats will come begging to take me to some piss-hole for a lay. Now I don't want a whore, you understand? I just want a nice, presentable girl who'll go dancing with me . . . a senhoreeta, sabe sabe?"

My chest ached, and I knew I was going to cry.

"Oh, balls!" Murray pushed back his cap and dug into his

shirt pocket. "Here's two U.S. greenbacks. Understand? *American* dollars. Take them." He forced open my hand, slapped in the folded bills.

"They won't go out!" I shouted, tears starting down my face. "They don't go out with strangers."

"Balls, kid. You just tell them I got plenty of moola. Plenty more where that came from." His voice softened. "Now look, Howie, you take me to the store like a good kid." He squeezed my shoulders, squinted mulishly into my eyes. "Just point it out. I'll do the rest."

"No, Murray." I flung the bills at his stomach, and bolted.

"Hey!" he called, and started after me, but I ran hard, past El Gallo and its whining whores, past the F.D.R. posters in the Chinaman's shopwindows, past the Rex Theater with its cowboy titles and the newsstand with *Life* and *Time* and Lucky Strikes, then across Parque Concordia to Sexta Avenida and all the way to Father's store.

🞉

IN SEPTEMBER THE student demonstrations took a violent turn. I was in the Palace orchestra, watching the Saturday matinee feature, *Guadalcanal Diary*. William Bendix was on the screen, crouching in a bomb shelter, Lloyd Nolan and a boyish Anthony Quinn somewhere in the background. Bendix was in the middle of a soul-rending confession as Japanese bombs burst all around.

Suddenly the lights came on. The projector rolled on, but the images were faint. I was not lured from the screen by the commotion in the rear of the theater, not even when the doors flew open and let in sunlight. The sound track went, but still William Bendix was on the screen and he was—he was saying

132

something of tremendous importance, something that could make me strong, and good, and free. . . . The sound! Bring back the sound! The Jap planes are overhead and William Bendix is unlocking his heart. Where is the sound!

A hand seized my shoulder. "Come. We must go. *Manifestación.*" It was Edna.

"But the film—William Bendix . . ." I pointed at the screen, but it was now blank. Blank, emptied of emotion, I allowed Edna to drag me out of my seat and up the aisle. Only after we emerged into the blinding sunlight did my mind attempt the leap from the wholly real, sensible illusion of William Bendix and Guadalcanal to the senseless fact of a foot-stamping, placard-waving mob screaming, *"Muera Ponce!" "Viva la revolución!"*

I despised them and their revolution.

La Revolución

THE SHOOTING BEGAN SHORTLY after midnight on October 20, 1944. I awoke to the sound of firecrackers, thousands going off at once. I rubbed my eyes and tried to remember what festival this could be that started in the middle of the night. Carnival? That wasn't until February. Corpus Christi? One look out the window at the brilliant red flashes convinced me this was no festival, and these were not firecrackers. Bullets! The clanging on our tin roof. The dry rattle of machine guns. It was *Mission over Tokyo* and *Guadalcanal Diary* magnified a hundred times. Only this was real, it was happening

134

in our streets, not on the screen. I called to Becky across the room but she made no reply. Little fool, she was fast asleep. I turned to the window again, my eyes riveted to the orange-red tracers. They were headed north, toward the National Palace, just two blocks away. I covered my head with the blanket and pressed my ears, but the sounds were still there.

A loud rumble. A huge ghostly shape lumbered past, rattling the windows, shaking the house to its foundations. With a howl I leaped out of bed and ran toward Father's room. At the door I tripped over Eulalia and Micaela, who were huddled together, chanting prayers.

Father stood at his bedroom window, robed and calm, taller than I remembered. He was watching the tank go by. I seized him around the waist and would not let go.

He patted my shoulder. "Come. Back to your room. It is safer there. Where is Rebecca?"

"As-sleep." I could not control the chattering of my teeth.

"Calm yourself. It will pass." He unclasped my arms firmly, led me back to my room, and sat me on the bed. Then he went to fetch Mother. I looked again at Becky's inert shape under the blankets. "Stupid," I said angrily. "Stupid, stupid. Doesn't know, doesn't care, we're all going to be dead."

From the corner Eulalia and Micaela chanted Ave Marias, their faces flickering red.

Father brought in Mother, crouched small against his chest. She took one tiny step after the other, as if the ground were about to open and swallow her up. She was as terrified as I was, and more helpless. This was no comfort, but yielded a kernel of perverse satisfaction: It confirmed my low opinion of her.

The clanging on the roof grew louder. Now there were

135

isolated explosions behind the monotone stutter of the machine guns.

"They're shooting at the Palace," Father called from the window. "That means revolution."

Crouched on my bed in her purple chenille robe Mother rocked to and fro, like a mourner. "What shall we do? In the name of Israel, what shall we do? They will kill us all."

"When the shooting stops we must move to a safer place." Father's voice rose strong and calm above the din.

"Where?" Mother said. "Where can we go?" She looked up. "Isaac, for the love of God, get away from that window."

Father did not move. "To Perla's house."

"But we can't get out. How can we get out? Get away from that window, Isaac. They will kill us all."

"Calm yourself, Esther," Father said. "You are behaving badly." He sat on the bed beside her. "I don't mean now. We'll move out when the shooting stops. It can't keep up all night."

"The laundry room, *señor*. The laundry room has no windows. It is safer there." It was Micaela, looking up from her prayer beads.

"Yes," Father said. "Yes. We will move into the laundry room." He rose from the bed. "We will move there right now, one at a time."

I stiffened. To reach the laundry room we had to cross the exposed hallway, under a hail of bullets.

Mother said, "I do not move. From here I do not move."

"You are behaving badly, Esther," Father called from the window, to which he was drawn like a moth. "Calm yourself."

Mother rocked back and forth, unheeding. "From here I do not move."

Father took Micaela by the shoulders and led her into the hallway. In a moment he was back and led Eulalia across. Then he lifted Becky and carried her out, sound asleep. He came back, raised Mother by the shoulders, and dragged her out the door like a petrified shrunken old woman.

I made up my mind to be brave.

We were halfway across the corridor when a brilliant fireball blazed across the sky. A shattering explosion followed, very close by. My legs buckled and Father carried me the rest of the way.

We lay silent on the floor of the windowless laundry room, listening, in the lulls between machine-gun salvos, to the pounding of our hearts. Becky lay next to Mother on the room's only cot. She awoke once to ask what holiday this was. When Father said it was no holiday, but a revolution, she asked if this meant she wouldn't have to go to school. Father said it did. She turned over and went back to sleep. This was the first cheering news of this apocalyptic night. There would be no geography quiz that morning, or the morning after, or the morning after that. I had not studied for the dreaded exam, and now my delinquency would go unpunished.

Somehow, despite the chattering of my teeth, the spasms in my diaphragm, I dozed off. When I awoke a ribbon of greenish light had seeped under the door of the laundry room. The bursts of mortar had grown distant, formal, like the cymbals of a receding band. The rounds of machine-gun fire were shorter than the silences between them.

Father rose from the floor. "The shooting has let up. We can go out now." He instructed us to get dressed and gather one week's change of clothing.

The sun had risen behind the National Palace—miraculously still standing—as we filed out the street door with our bundles and suitcases. We headed north on Séptima Avenida, hugging the walls like pack rats. Father was at the head, with Becky asleep in his arms and Mother behind, clinging to his coattail. I was next, followed by Micaela. Eulalia had volunteered to stay behind and look after the house, at least for another day.

To my amazement not only the Palace but all our neighbors' houses were still vertical, although some walls were lightly pockmarked. The gray streets were not littered with corpses. The cross fire, too, had been a *manifestación*, most of it high above the rooftops on a dialectical plane.

At the intersection of Parque Morazán and Sexta Avenida we passed a machine-gun emplacement. It was manned by five university students who grinned and waved as we went by. The shooting was over for now, and they lounged around their idle weapon, chatting aloud and breakfasting on fruit and a loaf of bread. They looked like a group of I.S. seniors on the big outing of the school year.

Jacob

AT AUNT PERLA'S THAT EVENING we heard over the student radio station that the rebels had won the day. In the south, Matamoros Fort and its key garrison had risen up against the government, as had the Guard of Honor citadel two blocks from the Palace. (It was their erratic shelling we had heard early that morning.) The government fort and main arsenal, San José, had been knocked out by a direct artillery hit from Matamoros. The broadcast went on to say that Provisional President Federico Ponce had capitulated that morning after a handful of heroic students planted a field cannon before the Palace entrance and threatened to blow it up.

Father hailed the news of Ponce's overthrow and said the country would now have its chance at democratic elections at long last. A bottle of Sabbath wine was opened by Aunt Perla, who was Father's younger sister, to toast the revolution's success.

Early next morning my distant relation Jacob returned from overnight duty on his machine-gun billet near the Palace. He looked scruffy, and his face was swollen from lack of sleep. His "militia" uniform—white shirt and black trousers—was rumpled and damp. But in Jacob's eyes shone an extraordinary radiance. I had never seen anyone more charged with vitality. When he carelessly squeezed my neck I felt the voltage right down to my toes, which left the ground. Seventeen-year-old Jacob became my new hero and instant savior.

Over a victory breakfast of his favorite Aunt Jemima *panqueques*, Jacob comported himself like a true revolutionary, pounding both fists on the table as he lectured Father on his party's program for a new constitution and social justice for the Indians, whom he called The Oppressed. Only after Father agreed in principle to his proposals did Jacob give us the latest news: Last night's broadcast, he said, had been inaccurate in one respect. President Ponce had not "capitulated." There had been no one inside the Palace to capitulate. Ponce, his sons, and his retinue of bandits and cutthroats had taken asylum twenty-four hours earlier in the Mexican consulate. The rebels had been firing all night on a virtually undefended stronghold: "an empty symbol," in Jacob's words, "of reactionary bourgeois decadence." As rendered by Jacob, all his loose scraps of hearsay, propaganda, and third-hand report amounted to a crushing rout of the enemy by the Popular Liberation Front.

In the ensuing weeks there were disquieting signs that Jacob's victory breakfast had been premature. The reactionary pro-Ponce forces staged a comeback, their ranks strengthened by entrenched supporters of Ubico. Threatened with civil war the new "revolutionary council" appointed a caretaker junta of two military and one civilian to govern the country until a new constitution was drafted and free elections could be held. The junta immediately disbanded the Assembly and the National Police as "fascist organs." Under a proclaimed amnesty Ubico's jails were emptied of prisoners.

Almost overnight the papers reported a sharp rise in violent crimes in the cities, towns, and provinces. The systematic slaughter had begun between liberals and conservatives, between *Arevalistas* and *Ubiquistas*, and among fanatic partisans of a half-dozen splinter factions.

After ten days at Aunt Perla's we returned home in the belief that the revolution had succeeded and the millennium was at hand. Father reopened the store, cautiously at first, two or three days at a time. But a gang of looters kept breaking in at night and he had to install an extra set of steel shutters and hire a night watchman. When the night watchman defected to the looters Father paid a trusted employee, Carlos, to sleep in nights. One night the looters broke in and roughed up Carlos so badly that he could not return to work. After that Father had no choice but to bargain directly with the looters and give them a hefty *mordida*, or bribe, to stop their looting.

School remained shut until February. I stayed indoors most of the day, reading and playing records, idly looking out the window at the army troops and the civilian militia patrolling the streets. One morning a band of Indian peasants trotted past my bedroom window, waving machetes above their heads and shouting, "Ubico! Ubico!" When he came home, Father said a reactionary leader had offered the peasants a few cents apiece to run wild through the streets and terrify the city, so as to pave the way for Ubico's return. The following day the same band of Indians trotted past my window, waving machetes and shouting, *"Revolución! Revolución!"*

Father concluded the other side had raised the bidding.

A machine gun was posted at our intersection one afternoon, to protect the Palace from reactionary terrorists who struck and ran. Jacob was one of the crew, on the noon-to-midnight shift. Jacob fancied himself a crack marksman, but the only time I saw him shoot his weapon he missed the target by a city kilometer. A car sped past the intersection scattering leaflets and bullets. By the time Jacob and his crew mounted the machine gun the car was long out of sight, and they settled for the satisfaction of perforating a few houses. Afterward Jacob bragged of this exploit as if he had scored a direct hit.

As with most student rebels Jacob became very popular in our neighborhood. We saw to it that the crew was well fed, and brought them warm clothing and bedding at night. Jacob looked ascetically thin and pale, but the fire in his eyes burned brighter than ever. "This is better than the books," he'd say, with an intoxicated laugh, when I brought him coffee or a bowl of fruit. Sometimes he would squeeze my neck, and the familiar charge went through me. But my toes no longer left the ground. I had begun to figure out it was not the revolution that intoxicated Jacob, but his idea of it.

The Brothers Bush

ON THE RARE OCCASIONS when I stepped into the street, I sniffed the anarchy in the air. There were no policemen to direct traffic, collect bribes, collar lawbreakers. In *El Imparcial*, an independent newspaper, graphic accounts of armed holdups and rapes competed with news of the coming elections. Thousands of citizens used the police vacuum to settle private scores. In the villages and towns many of Ubico's satraps were butchered by their former victims. Family vendettas turned into public shootouts and were blown up by the rumor mills into provincial "revolutions." Revolution was the order of the day, even among criminals. The civilian guard designated by the junta to maintain order made scant impression on veteran outlaws seasoned in Ubico's torture pits and penitentiaries.

In November the Indian marketwomen, a vocal and militant faction in the affairs of the city, staged a *manifestación* of their own. They shuffled down Sexta Avenida one morning, banging on pots and clamoring at the top of their shrill voices for a return to calm, so they could market their wares.

Elections were scheduled for mid-December. Weeks earlier a favorite candidate had emerged, Juan José Arévalo, an imposing educator with liberal credentials who had lived in voluntary exile in Buenos Aires for fifteen years. His long absence from Guatemala was Arévalo's chief asset. It protected him from the charges of collaborationism and corruption that were leveled against every other presidential aspirant.

With other enlightened members of the business community Father came out solidly in favor of Arévalo, praising him as a democratic reformer and imminent savior of the country's crippled economy. Father meant, I figured out months later, that Arévalo would be "good for business"; but by then, he wasn't. Still, Father's enthusiasm was genuine while it lasted. I heard him say many times that the revolution made him feel fifteen years younger.

By late November Arévalo was stumping the countryside with pledges of agrarian reform, massive literacy campaigns, social security for the poor—all issues that had been anathema only weeks before and would have been worth one's life to whisper in a public place. Popular support for Arévalo peaked in the final days of his campaign and then, ominously, declined. In the councils of the old guard conservatives who

145

controlled the economy—coffee planters, United Fruit executives, half the military—a chill had been raised by Arévalo's campaign slogan, "Spiritual Socialism." But there was no other candidate within reach of Arévalo, and he was swept into office with 85 percent of the popular vote.

He was the first democratically elected president in modern Guatemalan history.

School reopened in February, three weeks before the inauguration. For several days during this period two child rapists dominated the headlines. The Brothers Bush earned not only local but international notoriety by raping and murdering some two dozen minors, aged four to eleven. The elder brother, Miculash, was finally apprehended, "worn out by his travails," as one newspaper reported; he became the first public criminal to be executed by the civilian guard. The story went around that the younger Bush, who had accounted for only six or seven of the rape-murders, pined away in his jail cell, consumed with envy of his more accomplished elder brother, who soon became a legend.

In school we sang a jingle:

> *En mi casa me dicen*
> *El niño Bush*
> *Porque tengo las mañas*
> *De Miculash.*

At home they call me
El Niño Bush
Because I have the habits
Of Miculash.

A Show of Strength

ONE MORNING A PICTURE OF Coco Montcrassi appeared
on the front page of *El Imparcial*. He was in cub scout (*aguilete*) uniform, with one hand raised imperiously to an approaching car. In the other hand he clutched an ice-cream
cone against his breast. The caption under the picture read:
"Young patriot enjoys reward of service to his country in its
hour of need."

I dug out my *aguilete* outfit from the family discard-trunk
and rushed outside to direct traffic. By the time Father came
home at midday and scolded me for not asking his permis-

sion I had finessed across our intersection one ox-cart, five automobiles, a dozen motorcycles, forty to fifty bicycles, and countless pedestrians. One of the motorists had stopped to pat my head and deposit five centavos in my talented palm.

The next day was Sunday, and no traffic moved in our street. I quit early and wandered to Coco's post on Sexta Avenida and Thirteenth, just outside his father's sausage plant.

"I have been appointed Assistant Chief of Traffic Directors for this district," Coco called out, lofty and cool under his striped umbrella.

"Felicitations," I said, not the least surprised. I always knew Coco would go far. My eyes bulged, however, when he showed me his week's haul from public-spirited motorists: one police whistle, a tarnished police shield, an ocarina (plastic), a fistful of coins and bills amounting to three quetzales.

"That's very good," I said, adding with calculated understatement, "I can't do that well where I am. . . . I don't even have an umbrella."

"This is nothing," Coco said. "Tomorrow I'll be moved to Eleventh Street, across from the Lux Theater. There I'll really clean up."

I whistled. "Your parents won't object?" The Lux intersection was one block away, and rife with commotion.

"My parents grant me absolute autonomy," said Coco, parroting one of the slogans of the day. "They know I can look after myself."

Coco blew his whistle and signaled a right turn to a Buick

sedan. Into Coco's extended right palm the driver of the Buick dropped, as he slowed for the turn, a large silver coin. Without pausing to inspect it Coco closed his hand and pocketed the emolument, like a professional. "If you want," he said, twirling his whistle, "I can arrange with the chief traffic director to assign you this post."

"No thanks," I said, dejected. "Father wouldn't allow it. It's too far from home."

Coco gazed down from his shaded platform, and raised an eyebrow. "*Must* he know?"

I hadn't thought of this. . . . But no, it wouldn't work. "He'd find out. One of the salesgirls is sure to pass this way and see me." My gloom deepened.

"That is a shame," Coco said, "because—" He stopped in midsentence to signal a left-turning Harley-Davidson whose rider grinned at Coco as he revved by us, but gave nothing. "It is a shame, I say, because I had a proposition to make to you."

"Oh? What kind?" I was wary.

"I was going to propose you join me on the scout march next Sunday."

"What scout march?"

"Don't you read the papers?" From his back pocket Coco drew a folded copy of *El Imparcial* and opened it to a full-page announcement in the center:

Attention All Scouts: There is to be held a full-dress march through the streets of our Capital on Sunday March 11, 1945. All Scouts are to assemble in full uniform on the southeast corner of Parque Central by six-thirty a.m. on that date. Your partic-

ipation in this extraordinary event, in view of the present crisis
of our Republic, is vital and mandatory. For all further partic-
ulars contact

Your Scoutmaster,
Robert Urrutia, Lic. D.D.
Capital Chapter.

"What is the march for?" I asked.

"What do you think? Use your head." He tapped his left
temple.

"A *manifestación?*"

"Precisely. It is a show of strength to give criminal elements
the impression that public order has been restored."

"I see."

"It is an obvious ruse, of course, but it has its merits. And
it might work."

I read the notice again. "But this doesn't mention cubs. It
doesn't say *Aguiletes* are included."

Coco sighed. "Look again. It says 'All Scouts' at the top,
doesn't it?"

"True," I conceded.

" 'All Scouts' means *All* Scouts, which categorically and
by definition includes *Aguilas* and *Aguiletes.*"

I said nothing. One does not lightly contradict a logician
of Coco's caliber.

"Examine the evidence carefully," said Coco, signaling to
a cyclist, "You will see that my conclusion follows necessarily
and irreversibly from the premise."

"Granted," I said, "but it's out of the question. My father
would give me hell." I did not mention that I was no longer
a dues-paying member of the force. I had quit the previous

year after fainting twice on an expedition to the top of Pacaya Volcano.

Again Coco gazed down from his Olympian podium and raised an eyebrow. This time I guessed his drift.

We agreed to meet in Parque Central at six-fifteen A.M. the following Sunday. To forestall the embarrassment of a parental veto we decided not to seek their permission. We agreed not to mention the march at all.

I rose at dawn next Sunday, tiptoed to the laundry room and slipped on my *aguilete* uniform: short olive trousers and shirt, red scarf, olive cap. The first wisps of color had stained the eastern sky when I got to the park, where a dozen scouts had already assembled, tall, lean, consciously adult in long trousers. I sat down to await Coco on a tile bench, my lids drooping and teeth chattering from the cold. After fifteen minutes more scouts arrived and milled about, but there was no sign of Coco. The icy tiles raised goose flesh on my scrotum. I wondered desolately if Coco had been found out or had overslept.

By six-thirty I felt betrayed. I was debating whether to stay on my cold bench, small and unnoticed, or creep home through the labyrinth, small and unnoticed, when I heard a familiar voice from the crowd.

"Ey, short-pants, are you marching today?"

"Could be," I said, sitting up. I attached the taunt and its matching sneer to the pimply face of an I.S. sixth-grader, a notorious rowdy named Ortíz.

"Well, you will have to march by yourself then. You're too tall for the rest of us."

"Could be," I said, rising stiffly.

The scoutmaster blew his whistle and the scouts fell into

ranks of three. With Ortíz's remark still rankling I marched to the end of the column and formed an orderly rank of one.

The scoutmaster approached me, his whistle clamped between his teeth.

"Your name?"

"Nissen, sir, Jaime. At your service."

"Rank?"

"*Aguilete*, sir. Eastern district."

He twirled the whistle between thumb and forefinger. "H'm. I don't recall seeing you at the lodge." He said this weightily, as if he were about to unmask a cunning saboteur. "Are you in Cazeras's troop?"

"Yes, sir." I had, in fact, been in Cazeras's troop. But that was before the ill-fated expedition to Pacaya Volcano.

"But this march is for *aguilas*."

"With your permission, Don Roberto, the notice in the paper read 'All Scouts,' which categorically and by definition includes *aguiletes*, if you please, sir."

Don Roberto's whistle jangled on the chain.

"All right. But you will have to stay abreast of the platoon. Keep in mind, this is a serious march, not a parade. Do not expect to be nursed."

"Yes, sir—no, sir."

"The decision is yours." He backed away and made another count of his troops. I was still the odd number.

The whistle blew. Don Roberto shouted, "*De frente . . . márchen.*" The drummer struck up the roll and we started with a brisk stamp and step toward the mouth of Sexta Avenida.

"*Un . . . dos . . . un . . . dos . . . un . . . dos . . .*" Don Roberto barked the count with military precision. All the legs in step: a brushing tattoo against the pavement, stiff arms swinging in a smooth, even rhythm. And the drum— "plam . . . terraplam"—to provide the proper martial spirit.

We turned into Sexta Avenida in perfect stride, a single flawless engine. At once I heard the deferential murmur from spectators lining the streets. A rising swell lifted me up and carried me on its back. This was the moment I'd been waiting for since I was five years old.

We passed Father's store and the murmurs from the crowds turned to cheers. Coco had been right. This was a show of strength, a demonstration that sanity and public order had been restored. How could this help but inspire respect in the hearts of the most callous evildoers?

On the polished fender of a parked automobile the tops of buildings flowed past, like the panorama in a newsreel. . . . I snapped my straying eyes back to the precise midpoint between shoulder blades of the scout ahead of me.

As we approached the Lux Theater the cheers and exclamations rose in a single voice. The entire city had turned out to greet us! We were the army of liberation! At long last the months of anarchy and bloodshed were at an end. . . . Poor Coco, I felt no rancor toward him now, fast asleep in his coward's bed. I pitied him for missing this experience of patriotism—*real* patriotism. For the first time I felt at one with my country of birth, my homeland, Guatemala. Long live the Revolution!

The tops of buildings vanished from my fixed line of vision. We were in the marketplace, and the cheers from the crowds grew so loud I lost count and fell out of step. At the same time an irresistible curiosity overcame me. I turned my head slightly and strained my eyes to the right. Then I strained them to the left. They met with two solid walls of mocking faces and convulsed bodies. I looked again, in disbelief. There was no mistake. The cheers had turned to raucous jeers and hoots. The target of these jeers, and of dozens of pointing arms, was me. When I looked back I had fallen several paces behind the platoon. I realized all at once the spectacle I presented: knee-length trousers, spindly legs, the shortest in the squad by a head; and all of it lagging three yards behind in a now thoroughly demoralized rank of one.

I tried to skip back into step, but my heart was no longer in it. The illusion of oneness had been shattered. I was no longer a soldier but a straggler, laboring hopelessly to stay abreast of his betters.

Gales of laughter swept the length of the avenue, ahead of us and behind. We were in the slums beyond the Barrio Chino, where the city's poor and the squatters live. Behind us a band of urchins burlesqued our stride, sniggering obscenely. An object whizzed past my ear and struck the scout ahead of me. On the packed sidewalks the mood turned festive. Men and women danced and clapped their hands to invisible marimbas. Fathers hoisted giggling infants to their shoulders for a better view. Mothers vanished behind grille windows to fetch their children and were replaced by grandfathers with toothless grins. More objects whizzed by and rolled along the pavement. Shoe-polish tins!

An urchin tugged at the seat of my trousers as the crowd egged him on. I was six paces behind now and dog-trotting with a hand on my cap to keep from falling farther back. The urchins began to pester and poke the scouts up front, like a swarm of locusts. The scoutmaster ordered a jog-step—needlessly in my case, I was in full canter. An urchin leaped for Don Roberto's scarf, to the approving roar of the crowds. When a flying tin hit a Scout on the head, Don Roberto blew his whistle and outran his troops to shelter inside the railway station.

I could not get away for I was engulfed by a half-dozen squealing imps bent on tearing off my clothes. I flailed and kicked at them but they made off with my cap, scarf, belt, and the back of my shirt. Stripped of my last vestiges of dignity I dodged into the railway urinal and waited, crouched against the wall, for the crowds to disperse.

I made my way home along the city's back streets. When I arrived, half-naked and in tears, my parents and Coco were waiting in the hallway. Mother broke down when she saw me, and Father's gray face made it clear there would be no harsh reprimands; nor would it have mattered much if there were.

Afterward I demanded an explanation from Coco.

"Father," he said. "He caught me sneaking out the back."

I studied his face. There was no condescension in it now, nor the smug self-assurance. It was an eleven-year-old's face, very pale and on the verge of tears. Then I saw the telltale smudge on his lip.

"What is that on your lip?"

"Ice cream. Chocolate."

"You lied about your father."

"Yes. I had second thoughts last night, but it was too late to call you."

"Dirty coward." I gave him a shove.

"I am not," he said, and shoved me back. "I would have called you."

"Dirty Frenchy coward." I shoved him again.

We grappled and fell to the ground, rolling over and over, pummeling each other's sides.

"It was horrible," I said, pressing my knuckles to his throat.

"I know, I know," he gasped. "We heard on the radio."

We wrestled and rolled all over the floor, sobbing, no longer pummeling but clinging to one another in a tight embrace.

III

THREE
RETURNS

Coco—1953

I SAW LITTLE OF COCO after we returned to school. He was elected class president and his new activities kept him busier than ever. He graduated the following year with the top academic ranking. In June he entered the military academy, *Escuela Politécnica*, which grooms for glory Guatemala's future generals and most of its presidents. I feared that Coco's astonishing trajectory was pulling him beyond my orbit forever.

But our orbits shifted for different reasons entirely. In September 1945 we went abroad to live in Bensonhurst,

Brooklyn, where Becky and I enrolled in P.S. 197. Because of my accent and a substandard performance on the baffling Stanford-Binet, the dean placed me in the dim section of seventh grade (average I.Q. 87) with thirteen aspiring Golden Glovers and their molls. By year's end I had made an excellent adjustment. I was straight C in all my subjects except French, and could reel off on a dare the batting average of every Brooklyn Dodger.

Becky became a model student and buried her energies in a relentless pursuit of moral perfection. Our parents and all her teachers were raised to paragons of virtue, immune to criticism. I envied Becky her scholastic achievements, and the even tenor of her life, unaware of the rage gathering silently at the roots of her being.

A year after I graduated from ninth grade as captain of the cafeteria monitors, Coco Montcrassi left the military academy to enter the law department of San Carlos University. He had decided on a career in government. Two years later Eduardo wrote me of Coco's debut as an administrator in one of Arévalo's government departments. I was by then a high school junior, intent on making varsity soccer and writing for the school magazine. My I.Q. had jumped fifty-five points.

In 1953, at age twenty, Coco was named to a post in the government of President Jácobo Arbenz Guzmán, who had succeeded Arévalo. He was an administrator in the National Agrarian Council, which had charge of Arbenz's land-reform program. This meant, among other responsibilities, organizing peasant labor unions and overseeing the expropriation of untilled land from the United Fruit Company and its parceling-out to Indian farmers.

I was in Guatemala that summer and made an effort to

seek out Coco. The winds of revolution—the real thing—buffeted me from the moment I stepped off the plane. A customs inspector addressed me with a wink as *camarada* and slipped me past unchecked after he spied under my arm a copy of Ortega y Gasset's *Revolt of the Masses*, which I was reading for a social philosophy course. En route to my pension the cabbie tuned his radio to a Czech music broadcast dedicated to "our brothers in Latin America and their heroic struggle against the imperialist yoke."

On Sexta Avenida the traffic was heavier than I remembered, and there were stoplights at the busier intersections in place of policemen; but the shop windows had lost much of their tinsel, as if their owners had all been visited by the spontaneous insight that commercialism is vulgar and not to be flaunted. Everywhere I saw billboard ads for the national literacy campaign, with pictures of grinning, literate peasants.

At the store I found Uncle Mair mopey and dispirited. Business, he said, was rotten; what little there was had been robbed of its pleasures by the revolution. Haggling with customers was not only out of style, it was outlawed as a decadent bourgeois practice. The Ministry of Commerce saw to it that the new *precios fijos*—fixed prices—were rigidly observed. To compound the calamity the store's employees had unionized and were filing petitions for retirement pensions and a percentage of the profits. This last demand was especially galling to Uncle Mair because it undermined the *patrón-peón* relationship that was the bedrock, in his view, of economic progress.

"It is only a matter of time." Uncle Mair sighed and shook his head. "In six months they'll take over the store, and I'll join your Aunt Renee and my two sons in Paris. I'll be happily rid of all this." He swept his arm over the rows of well-stocked counters and textile stalls, and the twenty-three liberated salesgirls standing stern vigil behind them, like Marxist bridesmaids.

Coco's photograph appeared in the newspapers *El Pueblo* and *La Hora* at least once a week. He looked the same in all of them, standing flush to the camera in a gray herringbone suit with padded shoulders and no tie. His jaws are set in a menacing scowl, his hands locked behind. The blond curls are combed flat, to no avail; they spring up from his round scalp to betray his youth. (In my mind's eye a ghostly ice-cream cone hovers in the foreground, like a double exposure: "In eternal reward for services to his country in its hour of need.") Beside Coco stand a swarthy village headman with a lubricious grin; a drowsing Indian coffee-picker; or a snake-eyed Ladino organizer. None of them come up to Coco's shoulder.

Coco would not see me, although I called his office several times and left my name with his secretary. When I tried him at home, his father told me with a catch in his voice that they hadn't seen him in weeks.

I did finally see Coco one afternoon when he addressed a peasant rally in the park. His effect on the crowd was remarkable. I had never seen a group of Indians so united in a common response. They clapped hands and shouted, *"Si, si, señor!"* to Coco's every other exhortation. And yet neither his tone nor his words were inflammatory. Quite the contrary: Like all of Coco's pronouncements from my earliest recollection, it was a sober and balanced rhetorical exercise, couched in an idiom better suited to a graduate seminar than a political rally. His voice rose only once, when he berated the "recalcitrant coffee barons and foreign monopolies" who would not relinquish their fallow land, not even after compensation had been pledged to them by Arbenz in the form of government bonds. What little I detected of Marxist-Leninist dogma in the address was subordinate to its larger theme, which was a call not to arms but to solidarity and restraint.

That afternoon I understood Coco's calling: He was a master orator, a Cicero pushed by events into the political arena, where he did not belong.

The following year Arbenz was deposed by Lieutenant Castillo Armas's ragtag army of three hundred irregulars, with the blessings—and air cover—of Allen Dulles's CIA. The revolutionary cycle begun in June 1944 was now complete, and the "Guatemalan Spring" was over. Within a decade the Armas head had swallowed the Ubico tail, and a military strongman was again in the presidency. The conservative private sector that had helped to put him there immediately reasserted its power: Two of Castillo Armas's official acts after confirming himself in office were to abolish the labor unions set up under Arévalo and return to the United Fruit Company most of the fallow land expropriated by Arbenz.

That year one half of me ran away in anger to the mountains.

᙭

UNCLE MAIR WAS once again the strutting cock in his hen coop. Aunt Renee returned from her residence in Paris with their elder son, Henry, who was to help his father manage the store. At nineteen, Henry showed an introspective, con-

163

servative bent. He had dropped out of business school in Michigan and then spent a year in an Israeli kibbutz, where he had supported ultranationalist causes.

Soon after Castillo Armas became president, Coco was declared Enemy of the State and fled across the border, where he accepted a chair in a Central American university's Faculty of Law. In 1955 he gained admission to the United States on the initiative of an American university, which offered him a lectureship in Latin American History. There Coco met and soon after married the daughter of an Australian sheep rancher. It was from Chicago that Coco wrote me of Eduardo's death of leukemia.

He stopped to see me once while passing through New York on a lecture tour. I was giving a party on the eve of my departure for a year of graduate study in Spain. I sensed Coco felt ill at ease with my college friends. He began telling jokes: off-color jokes, ethnic jokes, political jokes. His poor English and worse accent made the punch lines come out all wrong, but the jokes were not very good to begin with. My friends snickered uneasily and Coco told more jokes at a faster and faster pace until the party died and everybody went home, except for Coco, who was spending the night, and a Barnard senior who lived with me during my parents' stay in Israel. Under the blankets that night she told me Coco had sounded deranged. I denied this angrily, and we had a quarrel.

Coco next did a deranged thing. He enlisted in the U.S. Marines. How he passed their security screen is a mystery. He was posted in Brooklyn for his basic training, near the Mitchell Air Base. His wife lived on a New York parkway, not far from us, but I never saw her or Coco, although I called them several times after my return from Europe.

In 1957 President Ydígoras Fuentes extended a selective amnesty to political exiles of Guatemalan birth. Fresh out of the Marines with a psychiatric discharge, Coco returned to Guatemala with his wife.

In January 1959, five days before I arrived in Guatemala on a short visit, Coco shot himself through the head while cradling in his free arm his six-month-old son.

I have lived ever since with two obsessions. The first is that I could have talked Coco out of it, had I arrived in time; and the second, that at the age of twenty-five, I had outlived my generation and survived myself as well.

Henry, Michael, Eduardo— 1971

I DID NOT RETURN to Guatemala again for twelve years. Coco's suicide had closed a chapter of my life, and I moved in a diametrically opposite direction. My graduate studies in Golden Age Spanish Literature, and later on in Far Eastern religion had drawn me toward Spain and then toward India, where, eventually, I married. I gradually lost contact with Uncle Mair, who wrote me in 1962 to say I had disgraced our religion and the family name by marrying a Hindu, and I was never again to set foot in Guatemala. He even threatened to influence the consul-general against me, if I disregarded his warning. This was pure bluster, of course, typical of Uncle Mair's style, but the Talmudic injunction against intermarriage caused me some reflection.

When I finally did return, in February 1971, it was to gather material for a political article and to offer belated condolences to Uncle Mair and Aunt Renee following their son Henry's gruesome death; one month earlier he had been torn in half by the propeller of a fishing skiff.

He and his brother Michael had been fourteen and ten respectively when I had last seen them in Guatemala. Even at that age, Henry had borne the onus of primogeniture with a precocious gravity, intent on living up to his parents' extravagant expectations of him. Michael, on the contrary, was ingratiating and sociable—a charmer like his father, and his pranks made him the enfant terrible of the new American School they had enrolled him in. Michael's impetuousness sometimes got the better of him; at age five he had dived head first into an empty swimming pool and suffered a lesion in his skull that would come back to plague him.

After I entered college, a watchful distance set in between Henry and myself, although we carried on a fitful correspondence, and I met him for lunch or dinner during his visits to the States. Michael and I were kindred spirits, and the bond between us survived the impediments of distance, the eight-year difference in our ages, and the fallout from family quarrels. A letter from Michael in Paris had spoken of Henry's growing political conservatism, and suggested wryly that Henry had taken it upon himself to atone for Michael's radical inclinations as well as for my own "offensive unorthodoxies."

I flew south from Mexico City during a thermal inversion. A blanket of thick, brownish smog stayed beneath us until we neared the border, when it thinned to a pencil line that gave way, as we landed in Guatemala City, to the pure translucent sunlight I had taken for granted as a child.

On the taxi ride downtown my pulse quickened when I caught a glimpse of Pacaya Volcano with a plume of smoke rising from its cone and black vultures wheeling overhead. Along Avenida Reforma the streets were clean and brighter than I remembered; the purple jacarandas and scarlet flame-of-the-forest were at their peak. There were the familiar landmarks, linchpins to my childhood: the signal tower on Séptima Avenida, a dwarf Eiffel with pretensions; the rows of greening monuments to liberators and reformers; the cranky orange-and-blue buses that had taken forever in getting me to the airport on Wednesdays to visit Milo.

We passed the barricaded military academy, and the tempo abruptly changed. Everywhere I looked—on the overpasses, outside banks, government buildings, foreign embassies— were angel-faced young soldiers and police with submachine guns on their hips. Radio patrol vans with wire cages—called *perreras* or dogcatchers—cruised up and down the main thoroughfare in pairs, as did army trucks crammed with olive-clad soldiers armed to the teeth. Guatemala had been under a state of siege and virtual martial law since November, five months after the election of Colonel Arana Osorio.

I arrived too late for my cousin Henry's funeral, which had been large, expensive, and heavily attended by ranking members of Guatemalan society and the government, including one of President Arana Osorio's sons.

Henry, a successful businessman and industrialist of thirty-four, had indeed become a staunch conservative, even by Guatemalan political standards. In 1969 he had campaigned actively for Colonel Arana Osorio, the antiguerrilla "Butcher of Zacapa," and for his slate of right-wing candidates. When Arana won the controversial election by a slim plurality, Henry was offered a Cabinet post, which he discreetly turned down.

I had seen Henry twice the year before his death, the first time in Edgartown, Martha's Vineyard, when he came to spend a weekend with us. He had been very jumpy, and spoke of going about Guatemala with a pistol and hand grenades in his pockets because of assassination threats from the far left. When I used the toilet late at night our defective water pump made a loud staccato noise that caused Henry to leap out of bed and into the living room, gray-faced and naked to the waist, shouting profanities in Spanish and pointing his pistol at imagined assassins.

I last saw Henry in New York City, four months before his death. He had lost weight, his hair was turning white, and I noted an unaccustomed remoteness in his eyes, as if he were unable to focus on near objects, myself included. He talked for an hour about heart attacks and how to forestall them. We did not discuss the worsening civil war in Guatemala or the recent kidnapings by leftist guerrillas of the German ambassador and two of Henry's close business friends. We did not discuss politics at all, and he never told me of the Catholic Honduran girl he had been secretly courting for two years, and of whom Uncle Mair would never approve.

In retrospect I understood something of what Henry, the "good son" of the family had been up against, and I reproached him in death for not having confided in me. But I had not suspected then the intensity of the rivalry the family had encouraged between Henry and myself, pitting him, the responsible heir of the Nissen patrimony, against the renegade "crazy cousin," as Aunt Perla, with her twisted smile, described me. When my first novel was reviewed favorably the year before that return, my stock had risen on the family chart—at least temporarily—which apparently provoked Henry to do some serious stocktaking of his own.

Soon after my arrival I spoke with one of three fishing companions who had been with Henry the day he died. He said their boat had run aground in a sandbar, and Henry and one of the others had gotten out to push from the stern. He himself was wading toward the prow when the boat, its engine open to full throttle, suddenly bucked. He heard a shout, followed by a horrible grinding sound. When he turned around Henry had already been sucked in by the propeller. His face was torn to shreds, his body ripped down the center.

I heard several rumors that week that Henry's death had been no accident but a veiled political assassination. His rightist friends hinted that urban guerrillas of the left-wing Rebel Armed Forces (FAR) had liquidated him for his support of Colonel Arana Osorio's presidential campaign, while his leftist acquaintances suggested the right had disposed of him because of his growing disaffection with the government's repressive policies. At first I dismissed the rumors as hysterical conjecture, but after two weeks in the country I questioned only which of the two versions was more plausible. In the twelve years since my previous visit Guatemala had sunk into a bloody civil war, marked by a steady and almost ritual acceleration of terrorist activities by extremist groups of right and left.

Uncle Mair's reaction when I walked into the store—our first encounter in twelve years—was to slap his hand on the counter. "My son is crazier than you!" he shouted. Stunned, I thought at first that grief had unhinged Uncle Mair's mind, and he had not acknowledged Henry's death. But I understood immediately after that he meant Michael, a pariah like myself, who had thrown over a lucrative position as an accountant for an acting career in Europe. At age thirty Michael had returned home from London, where he had scored no dramatic triumphs on the stage. He had grown his curly black hair down to his shoulders and wore sandals and Moroccan silk tunics. Michael, whom I had not seen in several years, was leading the improvised, marginal existence of a "jippie," one of the very first, and most conspicuous, in Guatemala.

"My son is crazier than you!" And an open-handed slap on the counter. Unhinged or not, the gesture was quintessentially Uncle Mair's, and it instantly reasserted his avuncular authority. His thick head of hair was spun white, his eyes were glazed and sunk into their sockets, the loose folds of skin under his chin shook from the impact of the slap. At age seventy-one, and over the brink of senility, he was struck down with grief, but the presence was still there. To my adult eyes Uncle Mair was undiminished in size; if anything, the senseless death of his elder son and the alienation of his younger, and favorite, had invested him with a tragic dimension.

The salesgirls reacted to my entrance like a chorus of Greek keening women, forever in anticipation of a tragedy worthy of their roles. I felt their concentrated gaze on us as Uncle Mair pressed my shoulder in a tentative *abrazo*, and tears sprang to his eyes.

"He is crying again," the murmurs rose from the rear of the store, gathering in volume as they reached the cashier's platform where the stricken patriarch, my uncle, still held sway. "Don Mair is crying again. His nephew's arrival has unsettled him."

I greeted each of the twenty-one salesgirls, singling out for a warm embrace the eleven survivors from my father's time. And more tears flowed.

"You are needed here now," said Marina, who had fondled me on her lap when I was an infant. Her hair was almost as white as Uncle Mair's, but she was motherly-buxom and as soft as I remembered. Marina had never married; she had remained a faithful consort to my father and Uncle Mair.

"You are needed by your uncle and aunt. Your cousin Henry is gone, Michael is lost, lost beyond help. He has grown his hair long, like a jippie, he lives with a divorced town-woman and they smoke marijuana in public. You are needed here now. This tragedy has broken your uncle's heart."

As I was leaving the store Choma, a shy and spectrally pale spinster who had been with Father since the early twenties, blocked my exit.

"The family name must not die," she said, shaking, her knuckles white against the counter. "There must be an heir and he must be a son."

I assured Choma there would be an heir, in time. She praised the Virgin, blessed me, and let me pass.

The next day I had lunch with Edna, my old favorite, who had quit the store years before out of loyalty to my father. At forty-seven Edna was thick-bodied and matronly, but her distinct Mayan features were untouched.

"I am a Christian," she began, in the high, lilting voice she had used for telling bedtime stories. "As a Christian I believe that this tragedy is a punishment on your uncle and aunt for the way they mistreated your parents. Before his death your father confided to me how your uncle had cheated him out of a large share of his capital. You were in Europe then, so you probably did not know of this. Your aunt is a woman of expensive tastes, as you know, and she always had to have the best and most costly in cars, clothes, and everything else. And your uncle paid for these extravagances by cheating your parents of their rightful income from the store. Your father was a good, generous man, even though he wasn't a Christian, and that is why we all loved and respected him. Your uncle won us over for a time with his masculine manners and his humor, but most of us learned to see through him. I think he is a weak man, governed by the whims of Doña Renee, and may the Holy Virgin forgive me for saying so." Edna crossed herself twice, and we talked of something else.

The week of my arrival I learned of the cowardly assassination of Adolfo Mijangos, a distinguished law professor and leader of the opposition in Congress. Mijangos, whom I had known slightly, had been paralyzed from the waist down in a car accident. He was machine-gunned in his wheelchair by right-wing thugs as he was leaving his midtown office. The next day Juan Luis Molina Loza, a popular philosophy student, had disappeared from his home, and was presumed dead by his friends. Both men had been moderate leftists, and were brilliant dialecticians. They had been immensely popular with university students, and had grown more and more outspoken in their criticism of Arana Osorio's "pacification" program and his suspension of civil liberties. Any one of these factors would have assured them a place on the right-wing death lists.

During my first weeks in the country, as the stories spread of atrocities by extremists of right and left, and the assassinations by vigilante death-squads steadily mounted, I began to comprehend the extent to which my acquaintances and friends had been brutalized by the prolonged civil war. But I was not prepared for the transformation in members of my own family.

"Mijangos was my classmate in San Carlos University," said Jacob, the same Jacob who had commanded a machine-gun crew during the '44 Revolution, and who was now a prosperous textiles importer. "We were friends for about a year, and he was undeniably a brilliant man, one of the most brilliant ever to graduate from San Carlos. But he fell in with Marxists after he traveled abroad, to Paris, and he went bad." Jacob's brown eyes vacated, little gray shutters closed behind them. "Mijangos turned Communist in the Sorbonne. When he came back, he became the ideological brain of the guerrillas, and don't waste any pity on him because it doesn't matter how you get rid of such scum."

"That's right," concurred Isaac, his younger brother, who was my host that first week. "Don't be fooled by his wheelchair. He would have done exactly the same thing to the other side." More little gray shutters, like the iron screens on Jacob's shop windows, snapped shut behind glazed eyes.

That night, for the first time since childhood, I wept aloud in my sleep. The following night I slipped into the darkened room of Isaac's kitchen maid and stayed with her until morning.

I DID NOT seek out my cousin Michael until I had been in the country for almost a week, but I heard that several friends of his had been arrested on drug charges during a police raid of a hippie hangout, La Creperie. By this time the extent of the violence had begun to sink in, but I had not yet acquired the shield of numbness that protected my relatives and friends, or the careless *machismo* of going about one's daily business, unflinching and unmoved, as the bullets fly about. I felt exposed, vulnerable, and also cursed, like a one-eyed man in the kingdom of the voluntary blind.

Another, less palpable violence confronted me as I searched for traces of my lost childhood in familiar landscapes and in the recollections of relatives and friends. I searched in vain. Not only the substance, but the remembered colors and textures of my boyhood had grayed and shriveled. It was as if a malignant cloud that hung just above the rooftops as I was growing up had descended at last, swallowing up the very air around the people I knew and converting them to pale, one-dimensional imitations. The prevailing climate made a mockery of my hardening conviction that political commitment of any kind landed one sooner or later in a hopeless predicament; the fact was, you landed there in any case.

My cousin Michael was living with a tall Frenchwoman, Irene, a former fashion model recently divorced. The evening we met, in Irene's ground-floor apartment, she drew the window blinds and passed around a joint of potent Colombian grass, as "Jesus Christ Superstar" played on the stereo. Irene's son and daughter, six and eight years old, sat up with us, giggling and chattering trilingually as they got high on our exhalations.

175

At around midnight Irene lit a candle and two fresh joints, and we all sat up to talk.

"Henry's death was no accident," Michael said. In the dim candlelight the planes of his face were sharp and hard like his father's, just as Henry's small and softer features had mirrored his mother's. "If it hadn't been the boat, he would have cracked up in his new plane. . . . Henry woke up every day with the expectation that he would be killed or kidnaped by the FAR. He knew he was a marked man, and yet he hadn't the guts to stand up to my father and acknowledge the woman he loved, because she was Catholic. That is the absurdity of Henry's life, and it is why I cannot absolve him of my contempt. Although he faced the daily threats to his life like a man, he cringed like a boy of nine in front of my father. At the age of thirty-four my older brother was a half-person, neither boy nor man." Neither grass nor the candlelight softened the haunted, half-mad look in Michael's eyes.

"Henry did not fulfill his life," Aunt Renee said, the day I visited her home to pay my respects. At sixty-one she was a slender, handsome woman, despite the dark hollows under her eyes and puffed cheeks from extended mourning. "He did not realize his ambitions, and that is why I can never accept his death. It's true my son had success in his career, he was extremely popular, he had all the material comforts and a little more besides. But he did not live long enough to enjoy the fruits of his success. Henry did not know real happiness, except in childhood. He never knew love for a young woman, a good, home-loving Jewish woman who would give him children. Instead, he threw away his youth on weekend fishing trips with his bachelor friends. Nothing, no one, can make me accept Henry's death." Aunt Renee rose from her sofa, dry-eyed and erect, to fetch us tea. The spacious drawing room we sat in, which she had converted years before into a gaming parlor, had been cleared of card tables and the television set to accommodate mourners. Cold, vast, and empty, it already resembled a mausoleum.

"I do not understand why my older son is dead, my younger one wasting himself on drugs and common tramps, and I have to go on living," Uncle Mair said, the afternoon I lunched at his home. "Who shall I leave everything to? The salesgirls? What good is a life, a prosperous business, if a man has no one to leave it to? I have no son, no heir, no successor. Why I must go on living, I cannot understand"—he sighed, covered his eyes—"only the will of God." After his noon siesta he took me aside and pleaded with me to spend a few days with Michael. "You both speak the same language. Perhaps you can persuade—no, not persuade—but just talk to him, understand his way of thinking, and find out if perhaps, later on, he might be persuaded . . ." His voice broke off, he waved his hand in the air, covered his eyes. We did not speak of Michael again.

"The week I arrived from London I organized a street theater group with some friends . . ." Michael and I were having our afternoon coffee in a pastry shop midtown, and I could feel every eye in the crowded room slide down Michael's long hair, light onto my own medium-length cut, and prick my neck, like stinging ants. How long before one of those eyes—any one of them—would slide along a gunsight?

"Six of us gathered in Parque Central one afternoon and replayed in pantomime the 1954 overthrow of Arbenz by Castillo Armas and the CIA. You know, one of us played Eisenhower, another Castillo Armas, a third U.S. Ambassador Puerifoy, and so on. We mixed it up a little, made faces at the crowd, shouted, 'Bang bang you're dead,' called each other 'Fascist pig' and 'dirty Communist.' Simple stuff, really, elementary street theater, not even Artaud."

Michael tossed back his long locks and smiled, mocking my signals to lower his voice. "About a dozen people stopped to watch. One of them was a National Police guard in full uniform, and another a plainclothes pig who took notes. The following day Rico, Pepe, and El Chino were picked up in La Creperie on phony drug charges—the pigs had planted the grass in their pockets—and they were taken to Pavon Penitentiary. No arraignment, no trial, nothing. Rico, who is seventeen, got out a week later with a broken wrist; Pepe, after two weeks, and he hasn't been right in the head since. Chino, who had been picked up once before at a pop music concert—Chino is still inside. Rico said he saw him being tortured—heavy stuff, like genital-squeezing, picks under the nails, the stinging-ant powder, and worse."

"What about you?"

"I wasn't picked up. It must be because of Henry. I felt very bad about it, but I imagine they'll get to me eventually. I've been videotaping mental hospitals, police barracks, Indian villages, and I know a jail guard who can get me into Pavon Penitentiary, for a price. I'm going to splice it all together and show it in the Lux Theater." His black eyes brightened, and he laughed. "It should be a real gas."

I asked, "Who'll pay for it?"

"I'll raise the money somehow, even if I have to steal it."

Later I discovered that Uncle Mair had given Michael $10,000 for the videotape camera, on condition that he show up in the store twice a week and dine at home on Friday evenings.

The following morning Michael took me to meet Claudia Lozano, Henry's lover. She was a small, pretty but not at all frail only daughter of a prosperous family, which she described as "Progressive Catholic."

"In the past year Henry had been tense and unhappy," she said, "and there was very little I could do. He was nervous about the FAR and the repeated assassination threats, but he had learned to live with them, with my help. What made it difficult was his uncertainty about his father's attitude toward me, and there I could not help him. He would make up his mind to speak to Don Mair about me and make a clean breast, but he always backed away at the last moment. Once he hinted about our situation to his mother, thinking she would be more sympathetic, but she ignored the hints and pretended not to understand.

"When Henry bought his new Piper Cub we flew together all over Central America, and he took me to Miami once. But he would not introduce me to his family, and I told him finally it would be better if we parted, and I gave him his liberty." She bit her lip. "I think Henry simply lost the will to live."

From her pocketbook Claudia took out a photograph she'd taken of Henry as he lay flat on his back at the beach. Large dark glasses cover his eyes and half his cheeks; his hands are crossed on his bare chest. His small, white face looks embalmed.

"That was taken a month before the accident," Claudia said.

Michael put down the photograph and passed a hand over his eyes. "My God," he said. "My God."

❀

ON THURSDAY EVENING I was visited by Eduardo Rodriguez's mother, Pilar, his grandmother, Tonia, and Julio, his younger brother. Noño had died three years before and the family had moved out of the quarry and into the capital, except for Tonia, who stayed behind to watch over Noño's grave. Eduardo's two surviving sisters were living in Mexico, married and raising large families.

"There is too much wickedness in the country today," Tonia said, seated small but erect on Isaac's electric-blue Danish modern divan. Her hair was still long like a village girl's, but it was pinned up in a grandmotherly bun. "People are turning more evil every day. I am almost glad Noño did not live to see the worsening. He would have been discouraged."

Inevitably the conversation turned to Eduardo, whose death after sixteen years seemed to have lost none of its impact. Julio, now twenty-five and employed as a bookkeeper in the same bank where Eduardo had only been cashier, criticized Eduardo's widow for having remarried less than a year after his death.

"It was not proper," he said. "It was an offense to my brother's memory. The flowers on his grave were still fresh."

"That is why we cast her out of the family," Pilar said, "even though she is the mother of Eduardo's only son." Pilar's eyes still had the yielding softness, but most of her teeth were gone and her hair was as gray as Tonia's. She spoke of Eduardo as if he had been her husband as well as her son. Eduardo's father was not mentioned even once.

180

As I spoke with Julio I felt he was a better person in significant ways, and more generous, than Eduardo had been. He seemed stabler, no less intelligent, and I saw none of the hard cruelty in his eyes. Before they left I tried to tell him this.

"Eduardo was my best friend," I said, and I heard my voice rise. "But I always felt there was a blackness in him. I felt Eduardo had made a pact with death. You must not let his memory stifle your own life and your career."

"Eduardo was a real man," Julio said, dully, without meeting my eyes. "I will never be able to fill his place."

I appealed for support to Pilar and Tonia. "Help him," I said aloud. "Help your son, Julio!" But Pilar's and Tonia's faces were set, their eyes glazed like everyone else's, and I was shouting to penetrate my numbness. Julio's verdict on himself was theirs as well. The process that had destroyed Eduardo's father and burnt out Eduardo before he was twenty-one was consuming his only brother. The women of the house had taken revenge on their men by compelling them to live out their myths to their inescapable consequences.

Mala Saña—
1981

ON THE AFTERNOON OF my next return visit to Guatemala
as an adult in January 1981, I went jogging in the large estate
behind my cousin Michael's iron-fenced town house in Villa
Hermosa, a fashionable suburb, and ran into two soldiers
with mongrel bloodhounds on a leash.

"Exercising?" one soldier asked, with a glance at my track
suit.

"Yes," I replied, slowing to a walk. "But I'm out of breath."

"Rest a while, then," he said, smiling, "and don't trip over
any corpses."

When I reported my encounter to Michael, who was my host during my first weeks in the country, he paled slightly. "Yes, I meant to warn you. The finca has become a dumping ground for the death squads."

In the decade since my previous extended visit, the war in Guatemala between the guerrillas and the latest in a succession of brutal military dictatorships was escalating out of control, fueled by the Sandinista victory in Nicaragua and the raging civil war in neighboring El Salvador. Twenty to twenty-five corpses appeared every day on city streets, in volcano slopes or rivers, or in one of dozens of clandestine cemeteries at the bottom of the small ravines that crisscross the Indian highlands. The differences between the violence of '71 and the bloodshed of winter '81 were more than statistical, as more and more Indians joined underground peasant unions and guerrilla groups, and appeared on anti-Communist "death lists" in regional newspapers.

In the capital, corpses was one of the chief topics of conversation among Michael's affluent friends in the upper middle class, which had suffered its share of kidnapings and assassinations. Twenty corpses a day, 500 to 600 a month, was too large a number for a republic of seven million to absorb without suffering severe internal dislocations. *"Ya no se compone"* (It's beyond repair), a phrase I had heard sporadically in '71, had become a litany among Guatemalans of all social backgrounds and political persuasions.

"Our violence is a consequence of our underdevelopment," a business partner of Michael's said to me the week I arrived, "and corpses are one of its chief by-products. We have many corpses, but at least they are biodegradable, unlike your nuclear waste."

During my stay in the country I listened to otherwise rational friends and former classmates who are now successful lawyers, doctors, bankers talk of *mala saña*, a fury that surpasses the *mala sangre*—bad blood—that accounted for the vendetta murders of a decade ago. *Mala saña* is a condition beyond motives of revenge, beyond all considerations of ideology or personal honor. It is a rage in the marrow that carries everything in its wake. When a loved one is murdered, relatives no longer make any effort to find out who did it, or why. *Nunca se sabrá*—it will never be known—is the ritual response, delivered with a tight-lipped shrug and a shake of the head.

In traditions that are far older than Westerners' preoccupation with nuclear annihilation, *mala saña* might well have been regarded as the eleventh plague, or the fifth horseman of the apocalypse.

❦

IN JUNE 1971, after my report on Guatemala had appeared in an American magazine, President Arana Osorio's private secretary had denounced me on the government radio as a troublemaking "pseudo-Guatemalan"; the secretary had later hinted to Uncle Mair that if I returned during Arana's presidency I would be chopped up into *picadilla* (native cole slaw). I naturally heeded this warning and did not visit again until the week following the devastating earthquake of February '76, when the more moderate regime—by Guatemalan standards—of President Laugerud García had replaced Arana's.

During my brief stopover in Guatemala after the earthquake, which killed more than 22,000 Guatemalans of Mayan Indian descent, I kept a low profile and was able to visit many of the devastated towns and villages in the highlands. I wrote for an Argentine publication of the courage and resilience I witnessed among villagers whose homes were destroyed and whose families were wiped out and who were able nonetheless to resume their lives within hours of the catastrophe, rebuilding tile and adobe huts and staging mass marriages of surviving sons and daughters "to recover the departed," as they said again and again. In the capital, where the earthquake damage had been minor, many of my relatives and friends had been severely traumatized, and provided a booming business for therapists and Valium dealers.

One effect of the earthquake had been to turn my cousin Michael away from the dissolute life he was leading in a hippie community in Santiago, Atitlán, and to return him to the family fold. Like many of his surviving contemporaries from the sixties' counterculture, Michael went straight in his early thirties, and he took his older brother's original place as bookkeeper for Uncle Mair's business.

In 1980, soon after the Sandinista forces ousted Somoza in Nicaragua, Michael married a South American diplomat's Gentile daughter and settled down to raise a family. When he wrote me that she was nine months' pregnant, I dropped all other plans and traveled to Guatemala to celebrate the arrival of the first male heir of our generation to carry on the family name.

At thirty-eight, Michael lived almost entirely from bank interests and rentals. Three years after the earthquake, which had miraculously spared the decaying old department store, Michael had finally persuaded Uncle Mair to liquidate the business and convert the capital into several large warehouses.

Michael and Consuelo hailed the birth of their son, David, as a kind of salvation—a testimony to life's resilience in the midst of the worst violence in Guatemala's turbulent history. And Michael threw himself into domesticity as fervently as he had formerly embraced radicalism and drugs. Michael went to his office only once or twice a week—in part because of the baby, but mostly because of the kidnapings. In the previous six months five of his close friends had died violent deaths. Alberto Habie, a popular leader of the Jewish community and head of the chamber of commerce, was machine-gunned in front of one of his factories by guerrillas of the Communist Workers Party. Another victim was the son of Michael's lawyer, who got mixed up with the underground. When I asked Michael whether he'd been killed by the right or the left, he replied, "What's the difference? He gambled his life, and lost it."

After three of his friends were murdered in a single week, Michael developed migraine headaches and stayed home all day long with Consuelo, the baby, and their Quiché Indian maid, watching Spanish-dubbed reruns of "Dallas" and "Barney Miller" on their color TV.

In February 1984 Michael suffered a cerebral convulsion, and traveled to Houston for a thorough physical examination. But the CAT scan found only some old scar tissue in the lining of his skull, left over from the swimming pool incident. Michael lives with the prospect of a recurrence, and no medical safeguards to predict or prevent it.

Uncle Mair sits every morning in his son's office, shaking his full head of silver hair over the atrocities he finds in the Guatemalan newspapers. After he sold the department store he had managed for forty years, Aunt Renee had prevailed on him to give up the empty old house haunted by Henry's bizarre early death and move into a large apartment nearer his surviving son's office.

Having won the battle for Michael's soul against drugs and Gentile seductresses, Uncle Mair had weathered his marriage to a Catholic diplomat's twenty-four-year-old daughter unexpectedly well. The birth of David, who looks the spit and image of his grandfather—down to the prominent Levantine nose—had melted any lingering resistance, and Consuelo was fully welcomed at the Sabbath table, in spite of her decision not to convert.

"Consuelo is a fine daughter-in-law," Aunt Renee says softly, looking pale and subdued across the Sabbath table. "And little David has brought the first sunlight into our lives since the tragedy. But too much of my life has ended with Henry's passing and your uncle's condition, which requires my constant attention, day in and day out. Nothing can rekindle the light that went out the day Henry died."

Since the kidnaping and murder of several Jewish businessmen Uncle Mair's symptoms of senile dementia have worsened. Every morning he asks the driver of his car to take him to "the house by the windmill," in Jerusalem, where he was born.

On his eighty-first birthday Uncle Mair's three Jerusalem sisters sent him a cassette tape crammed with old Ladino songs and pungent reminiscences of their impoverished but proud Palestinian youth. *"Ti ricodras*—do you remember— *Mairico,"* Elsa the eldest asks in Ladino, "how cold it was that winter, and you had to run barefoot through the snow?" Rachel the youngest follows with a gentle rebuke, punctuated with sighs. "All is forgiven, older brother. You are the only one left to us and we pray every Sabbath that you will come home soon to receive your blessings." And the middle aunt, Smadar, adds pointedly, "You know your place is here in the family gravesite on the Mount of Olives, across from the Golden Gate. Think what a pity it will be, Mairico, if the Messiah finds you buried on foreign soil."

The voices of the three aunts are as melodious and sturdy as on the evening they read me Great-Grandfather Yitzhak Moshe's biblical testament, in Aunt Elsa's apartment.

Uncle Mair plays the tape again and again, singing along with his younger sisters, nodding his head and talking back at them, as his eyes fill with tears.

❀

MY LAST WEEKEND in Guatemala I held a stag party for former schoolmates in the International School.

A few days earlier I had revisited the school and found it exactly as I remembered but for its shrunken scale, which made me feel like a Gulliver trespassing on his childhood. The stoop-shouldered and cranky registrar, who recalled me as a quiet, undistinguished boy, but good in languages, escorted me around the building, cackling senilely as he snatched up small boys who stood in our way, and boxed their ears. "After four!" he barked at the insolent ones who slipped from his grasp, just as he had forty years earlier. Every dark corner of the building, every room, every tile on the floor evoked a memory: the dank enclosed patio we used as a gymnasium, where I had suffered uncounted humiliations; the pillared corridor where we performed penitential knee-bends and push-ups when we were rowdy; the recess patio with its colonial fountain and the pre-Columbian toilet where Miss Seltzer had reputedly been raped.

The school had long ago reverted to civilian status but the discipline was as harsh as ever and the boys' faces were jarringly familiar.

Despite the curfews, all but one of my former schoolmates I'd invited showed up. There were four doctors, two engineers, two lawyers, a commercial photographer, an architect, an importer, a truck-fleet owner, a supermarket manager, a nutrition expert and an alcoholic, who was unemployed. Another classmate, a conservative congressman, never answered my telephone message.

The first to show up was Arturo Sánchez, my old tormentor and class bully. He was already high, and drank two quick Scotch-and-sodas before the next guests arrived. Arturo, who had grown into a short, thick-bodied mestizo autocrat with red-stained hooded eyes, is a surgeon and administrator with a powerful government institution. More than half of our two-hour reunion the week before had been spent on a scathing denunciation of three other classmates, all doctors, who had been trained abroad. Arturo, who had stood number two in the class rankings, had been especially venomous toward the number one, Gerardo Gutiérrez, a reputable nutritionist and obstetrician who had graduated with honors from Johns Hopkins University.

"They are all three unpatriotic," Arturo began again, sitting down and crossing his thick legs after pouring himself another drink. "If you're educated and trained abroad, then you should stay abroad. Let the *gringos* profit from their skills, meager as they are. I am a native Guatemalan, a *chapín* of part Indian ancestry, and I take special pride in my mixed blood. I was born here, trained and educated here, and I return the fruit of my education to my compatriots, who need it more than the *gringos.*" Arturo quaffed his third drink, and took a new tack.

"I am not like Gerardito, Angelito, Guntercito, two lily-white Spaniards and a pampered Kraut, whose parents can afford to send them abroad to be trained by *gringos.* I have supported myself from the age of twelve, and if I am where I am, it is through my own merit and personal sacrifice, and not because I have rich parents with connections in Juan Jopkins." He smiled slyly, narrowing his red-stained eyes. "In a few years I will be head of surgery in the government, and I will have something to say about who gets licenses to practice medicine in this country, and who doesn't. Then we shall see just how far rich parents, foreign training, and all these other little privileges get you."

As the other guests arrived, Arturo greeted them by their school nicknames or diminutives. I poured large drinks for everyone and they sat or stood tensely around Arturo's central chair, each conscious of his relative importance.

"Looks like old pear-shape has put on another twenty-five pounds," Arturo said, with a smirk, as the truck-fleet owner minced in. "He looks even more eunuchoid than he did in school. . . . And look at Angelito"—he winked maliciously—"the same white little hands he used to roll plasticine with, and his blue Harvard blazer to hide the rubber tire around the middle. Ey, Angelito, how many times was it you flunked out of Jarvard? Two or three?"

The importer raised three pudgy white fingers. "It was a record," he said, with a sporting grin. "The limit is two."

"So even your millionaire father couldn't buy you your Jarvard diploma?"

Angel's grin became strained.

Under Arturo's direction all conversation in the room reverted to fourth grade, the year he had reached the pinnacle of his influence over us by finishing first in the class. He had a remarkable memory: for the shape of Miss Dennis's legs when she turned to the blackboard, for the curve and size of Mateo Galvez's penis, and for the look on Miss Chavez's face the day she caught Mateo masturbating in the rear of the classroom. But most accurately of all he recalled each of our warts, deformities, our secret failures and perversions, and he invoked them at random to keep us in our places. It was true, despite individual successes, that most of us had grown fat, bald, frightened, sad around the eyes, but this was not enough to appease Arturo's animus. He had to remind Victor the architect of his preadolescent spells of diarrhea, so that his years of training and all his houses were flattened to the level of a malfunctioning sphincter. He accused Lorenzo the supermarket manager of kissing his father-in-law's ass, and Pedro the engineer of doling out heavy bribes to secure government contracts. León Gutiérrez, the out-of-work alcoholic, was reminded of his old fondness for patting boys' rumps during drill.

Not even the dead were spared. Arturo dismissed Coco Montcrassi as a "loony Bolshevik fag" whom neither the military academy nor the U.S. Marines could make into a man. And he insinuated that Eduardo Rodriguez's drinking and whoring had made him a discredit to *la raza*—Latins of Indian descent.

But the sharpest barbs were saved for Gerardo Gutiérrez,

who arrived late. "Gerardito," as Arturo addressed him, had recently left government service for private practice in obstetrics.

"Ah, Gerardito, Gerardito, my old rival, how I envied you when we were classmates. I loved you, yes, but I envied you more because you were number one, you were serious, and you were quiet in your seriousness because you knew in your heart that you were better than the rest of us. And now look at you, Gerardito, where are you now? Where did your number one and your internship in Juan Jopkins get you? What good was all the money your rich papa spent to get you a diploma? Look at you, Gerardito. You are bald as an egg, your paunch is spreading like a—like a malignancy, and you are so henpecked you had to leave government service to make more money for your stuck-up American wife and her shopping trips to California.

"What happened to your ideals, Gerardito? Where is your seriousness now? Remember, Gerardito, how you were going to help the Indian achieve dignity and equality? Remember that? You said the country could never free itself of its colonial past until the Indian achieved dignity and equality. And what happened to your research, Gerardito? Where is the miraculous organic meal you were going to perfect, so the Indians could eat like decent human beings instead of animals? That was the phrase you used, remember, Gerardito? And then you were going to solve the dietary problems of all under-developed peoples, wasn't that your plan? Ay, Gerardito of my soul, you are no better than the rest of us—you are perhaps worse, because you had the talent and the ideals we lesser mortals lacked, and you gave them all up to satisfy the whims of a ball-breaking bitch from California."

Gerardo stammered a protest, removed his lenses, and burst into tears.

Far from placating Arturo, Gerardo's tears goaded him into lashing at the rest of us with renewed energy. "I'll get you all," he hissed, his hooded eyes bristling, as we sat nailed to our seats, abject and numb, fourth-graders once more.

Michael and Consuelo, who had arrived from a party in carnival costume, retired in disgust to the rear patio.

"Where are your long-haired cousin and his clown companion going? To screw on the patio?" Arturo sneered. "How will they tell each other apart?"

Before I could reply León the alcoholic rose from his chair, pale, with both fists clenched.

"Shut your face, Arturo. You've said enough."

"Shut your own face." Arturo narrowed his eyes. "And while you're about it, why don't you join them on the patio? It never made much difference to you which end you got into."

León struck Arturo full in the face. To my surprise he made no attempt to defend himself, but sank to his knees, slavering and whimpering.

"I can't help myself," he said, as blood and saliva frothed in his mouth. "I can't help myself." His dark face sickened as he coughed and spat out blood. "I can't help myself."

He retched on the carpet, wiped himself with his sleeve, looked up at us with inflamed, rolling eyes. "You pricks all think you're better than me because you studied abroad and married foreign pussy. Because I have Indian blood in my veins you think that makes you better than me? You wait. I'll put you all in your places. I know your secrets, all of you. Not one of you can escape me."

I bent down to wipe Arturo's vomit from the carpet.

"And you, too." The surgeon leveled a finger at me. "You're an expatriate, and you've paid the price. But if you try to come back, I'll get you, too."